Rain followed behind h... feel solid under her feet. ... serious? It couldn't all ... could it? Thirteen years of living on the bus, always moving on from place to place. And if they did stop ... She felt her heart beating faster suddenly. She felt dizzy. Her head was swimming with possibilities. She hurried after Max.

Rain

PAUL MAY

CORGI YEARLING

RAIN
A CORGI YEARLING BOOK 0440 865158

Published in Great Britain by Corgi Books,
an imprint of Random House Children's Books

This edition published 2003

3 5 7 9 10 8 6 4 2

Papers used by Random House Children's Books are natural,
recyclable products made from wood grown in sustainable forests.
The manufacturing processes conform to the environmental
regulations of the country of origin.

Set in 13/15pt Century Schoolbook by
Falcon Oast Graphic Art Ltd.

Corgi Books are published by Random House Children's Books,
61–63 Uxbridge Road, London W5 5SA,
a division of The Random House Group Ltd,
in Australia by Random House Australia (Pty) Ltd,
20 Alfred Street, Milsons Point, Sydney, NSW 2061, Australia,
in New Zealand by Random House New Zealand Ltd,
18 Poland Road, Glenfield, Auckland 10, New Zealand,
and in South Africa by Random House (Pty) Ltd,
Endulini, 5a Jubilee Road, Parktown 2193, South Africa

THE RANDOM HOUSE GROUP Limited Reg. No. 954009
www.**kids**at**randomhouse**.co.uk

A CIP catalogue record for this book is available from the British
Library.

Printed and bound in Great Britain by
Bookmarque Ltd, Croydon, Surrey

To Ellie

'Stop it!' Rain said. 'Please, both of you, just stop.'

The row had erupted just as they'd started to leave, and now she was caught in the crossfire of angry words flying between her mum and her grandma. They both ignored her. Rain looked miserably from one to the other. Max, her mum, was tall and furious. The tiny room was stuffy. It was over-crowded with furniture and ornaments, and Max seemed far too big for it. Grandma was lecturing her as if she was a little girl.

'It's about time you stopped being so selfish and started thinking about what's good for Rain,' Grandma said.

'All these years,' Max replied. 'All this time and you still don't get it, do you? It's my life, not yours. I'll do what I want. We're OK, aren't we, Rain, you and me?'

Rain nodded reluctantly. She hated the way Max and Grandma always dragged her into their arguments. They only visited

Grandma once a year, and it always ended this way. They were at the front door now.

'Really!' Grandma said. 'Just look at that thing!'

The old red bus stood at the side of the road. It was their home. It had always been Rain's home, right from the day, thirteen years before, when she had been born on the back seat in the middle of a thunderstorm. According to Grandma, plenty of people had tried to persuade Max that living in a bus with a little baby was a crazy thing to do, but that hadn't stopped her.

There were crazy patterns painted on the sides that had been done by different people at festivals when Rain was little. She looked past the bus and saw curtains move in the windows of the houses opposite. Some of Grandma's neighbours were sneaking a look at them as they walked down the path, and others were staring openly from their gardens. 'Don't worry, Mum,' Max said bitterly. 'We won't embarrass you any longer.'

'Maxine, wait,' called Grandma.

But Max jumped into the driver's seat and started the engine. Rain stopped, ran back to her grandma, and kissed her on the cheek. She stood for a moment, not sure what to say, almost wishing they hadn't come. What was the point when it made everyone so unhappy?

Max hooted impatiently. 'I'm sorry, Grandma,' Rain said, and she turned to get into the bus. She looked back when they reached the end of the street and saw Grandma, still standing there waving.

They'd gone about fifty miles when the noise began – a whining sound coming from somewhere deep beneath their feet. 'What *is* that?' Rain asked Max. 'It sounds serious.'

'It's nothing,' said Max irritably. 'The bus is old. It's always noisy.'

'Not like this, it isn't.' There was another sound now, added to the first one. It was like tinfoil being crumpled. Rain could tell by Max's face that she could hear it. Max thumped the steering wheel with her fist. 'I don't believe this is happening,' she muttered.

'Look,' Rain said. 'There's a garage.'

There weren't any petrol pumps, just a flat concrete apron with grass growing in the cracks. At the back of the concrete was a huge shed with a corrugated iron roof. There was a sign on the wall. MOORE'S MOTOR SERVICES. Next to the sign was another one. FOR SALE. A truck roared by on the main road and the bus rocked from side to side in its slipstream. 'Great,' Max said. 'A ghost town.'

Rain got out of the bus. She heard the sound of a radio coming from the shed. There was a chink of metal. 'No, listen,' she said. 'There's someone here.'

She left Max sitting in the bus and went round the side of the building. A big sliding door was standing open. Inside, a man was working on a rusty blue car. The engine was running, and he had his head under the bonnet. Rain went over to the car and listened for a bit. The man didn't look up. 'Sounds like the timing's out,' she said.

The man stood up, and banged his head. Rain laughed before she could stop herself, he looked so surprised. No one ever expected a kid to know anything about engines, especially not when the kid was a girl. The man rubbed his head, then he nodded slowly. 'You're right,' he said. 'Where did you spring from?'

Rain told him about the bus, and the noise.

'You saw the sign,' he said. 'I'm closed.'

'You're fixing *that*.' Rain pointed to the car.

'Trying to,' he said, 'and I need to get on with it, OK?' Rain found it hard to tell whether he was old or young. There were deep lines of worry on his face, and he didn't look as though he smiled very often.

'Just let us put the bus over the pit,' Rain said. 'I'll look at it myself.' She was bluffing. She'd always fixed small things on the bus, and she could change a wheel, but she knew that this was a lot more complicated.

'You don't give up, do you?' The man wiped his hands on a rag. 'OK, then. Show me this bus of yours. But I'm not sure I can do anything.'

When they got outside Max was sitting in the sunshine. She stood up when she saw them, and the man stopped. People always stopped when they saw Max for the first time. She was taller than the man, and her hair was short, black and spiky. She was wearing a pair of ancient overalls, covered with paint, all different colours. Her feet were bare.

'Do you live in this?' he said, pointing to the bus.

'What's it to you?' demanded Max.

'Only asking. I suppose you're one of them . . . what do they call you? New Age people?'

Max flushed. 'I'm not listening to this,' she said. 'You don't know anything about me. Nothing. Get in, Rain.' She muttered something far ruder under her breath.

'Max! He's going to help.'

'Forget it,' the man said, turning away.

'Max!'

'OK, OK,' Max called after him. 'I'm sorry.'

'*Please* will you look at the bus,' Rain said. 'Max is fed up. It's been a bad day. She didn't mean what she said.'

The man hesitated. 'I'll need to take it for a drive.'

'Do what you like,' replied Max. 'I'll wait here.'

The man got in and Rain followed. 'Max doesn't know a thing about engines,' she told him.

'But you do, right?' He put the bus expertly into gear. They didn't have to go very far. The noise was getting worse.

'Could be a wheel bearing,' he said, 'but I don't think so. I reckon it's most likely the differential. And there's something else about the gearbox, too. Doesn't feel right. I'll take it inside and have a look.'

'Is that you?' Rain asked, pointing to the sign on the wall of the garage. "Moore's Motor Services"?'

'It used to be,' he said, frowning. 'I'm Tony Moore. And you?'

'I'm Rain. And my mum's called Max.'

Half an hour later Tony Moore emerged from the inspection pit shaking his head. He told Max how much he thought it would cost to fix the bus.

'You're not serious?' she said.

'That's if you can find the parts,' he told her. 'It's old, this thing. Almost an antique. I'm sorry.'

'How much do I owe you for looking at it?' asked Max.

'Forget it. I haven't exactly helped you, have I? I'd better get on with this.'

'Can I leave the bus here for a bit?'

Tony Moore waved an arm towards the cracked concrete outside. 'Wherever you like,' he said. 'Now I really had better fix this car.'

Max reversed out onto the forecourt and then jumped down from the bus. 'What are we going to do?' Rain asked her.

'I don't know.'

'We can't stay here.'

'You think I don't know that?' snapped Max. A truck flashed past on the main road, and another, and another. 'I need to think,' she said. 'I can't think here. Let's walk. Look, over there.'

On the opposite side of the road, a narrow lane led off into the countryside. Max walked quickly, so that Rain had to almost run to keep up. They'd gone about a mile before Max said, 'We could probably find a new bus for less than it would cost to fix ours.'

'So? Are we going to do that, then?'

Max had stopped. She was gazing into nothingness. All around them there were fields, some of them yellow with corn stubble, some of them already ploughed. In the distance a cloud of dust followed a green combine harvester. The noise of the traffic on the main road was a quiet hum.

'Are we going to buy another bus?' Rain repeated.

'That's what I'm thinking about. Maybe it's a sign.'

'Oh, Max, come on!' Max *believed* in signs. She saw them everywhere: a crow flying across the road, the letters on a car number plate, the words of a song they heard on the radio – they could all be signs. The trouble was, only Max knew what the signs meant.

'Maybe . . . maybe it's time to do something different. Maybe we could try and find a house somewhere.'

'A *house*!' Rain was stunned. 'But you hate houses. You were going on about them to Grandma this morning.' She paused. 'Why don't we go back to Grandma's? Just for tonight.'

Max looked at her. 'I'd rather sleep in the hedge,' she said. 'And I don't mean a house like Grandma's. I mean somewhere we could grow some vegetables, keep some chickens. Somewhere with a bit of space so I could do some really big paintings.'

Max was an artist. She painted huge pictures of sky and rock and mountain. It was what she'd always done, ever since Rain could remember.

'But we can't afford it, can we?'

Rain knew Max got money for her paintings, but not *that* much, surely? All through the year the stack of paintings grew. Max kept them under her bed, at the back of the bus. Then in the autumn they drove into London and delivered them to a gallery. It was only two weeks since they'd delivered the last lot.

'We wouldn't have to buy a place. We could find somewhere to rent. I could manage that, I think.'

'But where would we go?'

'I don't know,' said Max. 'Come on, let's walk.'

Rain followed behind her. The ground didn't feel solid under her feet. Surely Max couldn't be serious? It couldn't all be over just like that, could it? Thirteen years of living in the bus, always moving on from place to place. And if they did stop . . . She felt her heart beating faster suddenly. She felt dizzy. Her head was swimming with possibilities. She hurried after Max.

First there were flat fields, then there were trees. They grew thickly, arching over their heads as they walked, like a green tunnel. When they came out at the other end, the light was dazzling. There was a green space, and a pond. Ducks flapped noisily into the air. Max sat down on the grass. 'I think I'll have a little snooze,' she said. 'Five minutes, OK? It'll help me think.' She stretched out and closed her eyes.

'Max!' said Rain. But Max paid no attention. Rain looked down at her sleeping face. What was going on in Max's head? Did she actually *want* to settle down, live in a house? If she did, why couldn't she just say so instead of going on about *signs*? Rain sighed, then walked over to the pond. Two startled moorhens splashed away from her, and as she watched them scrabble up the bank she caught sight of a chimney behind a dense screen of trees and bushes. She glanced back, but Max's eyes were still closed. She returned to the lane and soon found a narrow entrance, blocked by pink willow-herb and long, thorny bramble shoots. She picked her way through and a cottage stood in front of her, small and silent.

The windows were filthy, but Rain rubbed until she could see inside. The place was definitely empty. There was grass growing along the bottom of the door. There couldn't have been anyone here for ages. Rain shivered with excitement. This must be exactly the sort of place Max was thinking of. And it was right here, as if it was meant to be.

Rain hardly noticed the thorns slashing at her legs as she ran back down the path. 'Max!' she yelled. 'You've got to come and see what I've found.'

Max sat up, rubbing her eyes. 'I must have dozed off,' she said.

Rain grabbed her hand and pulled her to her feet. 'You won't believe it. Come *on.*'

But when they reached the cottage Max looked at it doubtfully. 'So it's empty. We don't know they want to rent it out. There isn't a sign.'

'We can ask someone, can't we? Why else would it be like this?'

There was a long black shed that Rain hadn't noticed before because of the ivy growing over its roof. Max walked over to it and peered in through the window. The shed seemed to go a long way back under the ivy. It was full of some kind of junk, heaped up in the shadows.

'It could be your studio,' Rain said.

Max didn't reply. She crossed to the door of the cottage and rattled the handle. The door swung open and they stepped inside.

The floor was made of worn clay tiles. A little green light filtered in through the leaves and the grimy windows. A sink stood against the wall, but apart from that the room was empty. Max sniffed. 'It smells OK,' she said. 'Hardly damp at all.' She opened a door beside the fireplace. A spiral staircase climbed and twisted steeply. The stairs led to a tiny landing with two doors opening off it. There were two empty rooms with little low windows that looked out over the garden.

'We could try and find out about it,' Rain said. 'Find out who owns it. We could at least do that, couldn't we?'

They went back outside. Rain closed the door and Max went over to the shed. 'I suppose this *might* make a studio,' she said. 'It's hard to tell.'

'And there's the garden. There's loads of room for chickens and vegetables.'

'Yeah, well, it's probably someone's holiday cottage. Come on. We'd better get back to the bus.'

* * *

It was late afternoon when they returned to the garage. As Max unlocked the door of the bus Rain heard a child crying. A woman was pushing a buggy across the concrete. Two little girls in school uniform trailed behind her. In the buggy, a child with curly blonde hair and a red, chocolate-covered face was screaming at the top of its voice.

'Tony!' The woman was angry. Her face was white, and there were red spots on her cheeks. 'Tony! You promised you'd be back by five.'

Tony Moore came out of the garage. 'I was trying to get the car fixed. I've got to take Dan to training—'

'Here.' The woman shoved the screaming child at him. 'They haven't had their tea. D'you think you could manage that, at least?'

Tony Moore started to say something, but the woman was already hurrying towards the road. There was a hiss of brakes, and a bus stopped. She climbed the steps and disappeared inside. It was like watching a film, Rain thought. The bus pulled away and everything was silent for a moment; the three kids and their dad were all standing there, staring after it. Then the little one started crying again. Tony Moore looked down at his oily overalls and held the little girl away from him.

'Here,' Rain said, 'let me.' She stepped forward and took the child from him. 'What's your name?' she asked her. 'You've been eating chocolate, haven't you?'

The girl stopped crying and stared at Rain. 'She's called Hayley,' said the taller of the other two. 'And I'm Kerry and that's Annette.'

'I'd better get sorted,' said Tony. 'You lot stay here a minute. Kerry, you look after Hayley. Go on.'

'It's all right,' Rain called, as he disappeared back inside. 'I don't mind holding her for a minute. Do you live round here?' she asked the girls.

Kerry nodded and pointed. 'Just over there. How about you?'

'In there,' said Rain. She could see Max moving around inside the bus. The girls obviously wanted to look. 'Come on,' she said, 'I'll show you.'

'Did your mum let you paint on here?' Kerry asked, staring at the patterns on the side of the bus.

Rain laughed. 'It wasn't me,' she said. 'I couldn't do that.'

The girls followed her inside. The front part was where Max worked. The walls were covered with splashes and stripes of paint where she'd tried things out, but all Max's brushes and tools and paintings were stacked neatly away so they wouldn't crash around when the bus was moving. Max was standing there now, looking at the tiny space. Rain knew she was thinking about the cottage. She was thinking about having a studio. 'I'm just showing them round,' she said.

Max stood back to let them by. She was miles away. Beyond where Max was standing there was a sink and a table and a cooker and a fridge. And then, behind a curtain, was Rain's room. Max's room was right at the back. Annette and Kerry were both staring, open-mouthed.

'You really live here?' said Annette.

'I've always lived here. I was born here.'

'It's like a house.' Kerry had reached the curtain. She pulled it back and saw the shelves, row after row of books, each row held in with a wire to stop them falling out when the bus went round a sharp corner.

Tony's voice called from outside. 'All right, kids? Come on. Time to go.'

'It's Dad,' Kerry said. 'Mum was really mad at him.'

'I could see,' Rain agreed.

'Where's *your* dad?' asked Annette.

Rain was startled. 'I . . . I haven't got a dad,' she said.

'You mean he doesn't live with you?' asked Kerry helpfully. 'Lots of people's mums and dads don't live together. And some people have extra dads. My friend Mary's got three.'

'Kerry! Annette! Come on!'

Rain looked out of the window and saw Tony with the buggy. 'I think you'd better go,' she said. It wasn't easy to get them to move.

'Can we come again?' asked Kerry.

'I . . . We're not staying here.'

'Where are you going?'

'I don't know,' Rain said.

They reached the entrance of the bus, and Kerry took Hayley from Rain's arms. Max was climbing into the driving seat. 'What are you doing?' asked Rain.

'You don't want to spend the night here, do you? We'll park up on that green. No

24

one'll bother us there.' She started the engine as the girls jumped out. Tony pushed the buggy up to the driver's window and tapped on it.

'You're never driving this? How far are you planning to go?'

'Not far,' said Max.

'Well, don't. Ten miles, I give it. Twenty, tops.'

Max was about to pull out onto the road when a school bus stopped by the entrance of the garage. A tall boy, about Rain's age, jumped out. 'Dad,' he yelled. 'What's going on?'

'I thought you were never coming,' said Tony. 'Just take the girls home, will you? Give them some tea. Then maybe the car'll be fixed in time for training.'

'What about my homework? How am I going to do that? Training's not important.'

'Just do what I say,' snapped Tony. Rain was startled by the anger in his voice. The boy turned away quickly, red-faced, and started to push the buggy across the concrete. Kerry and Annette followed him.

'Time to go,' said Max. She crashed the bus into gear and then drove slowly down the narrow lane. Five minutes later they stopped on the grass beside the pond, and Max began to cook brown rice and vegetables for tea. 'It'll do you good to have something decent to eat,' she said, 'after all that junk Grandma was feeding you.'

'Why do you have to be so horrible about Grandma all the time? She only gave me chips and ice cream because it was my birthday. She was trying to be *nice* . . .'

Rain paused. Something was happening outside. A small car was nosing in between the trees. 'Someone's coming,' she said.

Max sighed. 'There's nowhere to hide, is there? Nowhere they'll just leave you alone. It's probably a farmer. Let me see.'

This was what Rain hated most about travelling. Red-faced people shouting at them, telling them to move on. And then, maybe, coming back in the night, shouting, jeering, chucking things at the bus. It was why she'd wanted Max to get rid of the red paint and the patterns. 'Why should we?' Max had said. 'If people don't like the way our bus looks, well, that's their problem, isn't it?' Rain didn't agree about that. It seemed to cause nothing but trouble. But there was no arguing with Max.

And now a man was getting out of the car. He didn't look like a farmer. He was young and he had long curly hair. He was wearing jeans and a hooded fleece top. An ancient dog tumbled out of the car after him, a hairy grey thing with bright eyes. Max was already outside. 'Yeah? You want something?' she said.

'I'm sorry. I didn't mean to disturb you.'

'Don't then,' said Max.

The old dog shambled up to Rain and stared up at her from beneath shaggy eyebrows. 'He's nice,' she said. 'What's his name?'

'Leaf,' said the man, and Rain laughed. 'Yeah, well,' the man went on. 'It just seemed to suit him, somehow. Look, I only came over because I saw you earlier, looking at the cottage. It *was* you, wasn't it?'

'We didn't do any harm,' said Rain quickly. 'The door was open.'

'I know. I thought the estate agent might have sent you. Only, they haven't actually advertised it yet.'

'You see!' said Rain triumphantly to Max.

'You are interested then? It's like a sign or something.'

Rain glanced at Max and saw the

beginning of a smile on her lips. The man was still talking. 'I mean, it seems too good to be true,' he said. 'When I only just decided to sell.'

'Sell?' said Max. 'I wasn't really thinking of buying anywhere. We could afford to rent, that's all.'

'Right,' said the man slowly. He thought for a moment, fondling the dog's ears. 'Well, why not? That might work out just as well for me. Why don't you come over to my house? Have a cup of tea. We can talk. My name's Simon, by the way. Simon Tanner.'

They followed Simon across the green and down the lane that led out between the trees on the far side. His house, when they saw it, seemed to Rain to be growing out of the ground. It was low and bent, and the roof was thatched and covered with moss. Climbing plants covered the walls. 'It's a bit of a mess,' said Simon. 'I only moved in a month ago. My father died, you see. I was working in London, and I had to decide. Either sell this place, or give up my job and move here and try to make it work. It's going to be an organic farm. Only it's going to take more cash than I thought. Dad let the place go a bit before he died.'

'Is all this yours then?' asked Rain. 'The green, all these trees.'

'"Bells Green" it's called,' Simon said. 'And yes, it's all part of the farm.'

'Well, I think it's beautiful,' Rain told him. 'You won't pull the hedges down, will you? You won't make it all flat and bare?'

'No way.' Simon smiled at her. 'I like it like this. But it's going to be hard work, and I need money. That's why I was going to sell the cottage. Come inside.'

He opened the door and Max had to duck her head as she passed through. The kitchen was huge. An old black range was pumping out heat and a big table sat in the middle of the room covered in papers. A sleek, transparent laptop computer stood in the middle of the chaos.

Rain sat down at the table and picked up a big book that seemed to be all about chickens. Leaf came and put his head on her knee. Max and Simon were deep in conversation. One corner of her mind registered the fact that Simon was explaining all his plans for the farm, and that Max didn't seem to have argued with him yet. Which was pretty amazing, because Max argued with everybody.

'We'd better go,' said Max at last. 'We still haven't eaten.'

'But we haven't talked about the cottage,' said Simon.

'Yeah, well, we probably can't afford it.'

Simon said a number. It sounded like a huge amount to Rain. But Max just nodded. 'It might be all right,' she said. 'We haven't decided anything yet. We might even get another bus.'

'You don't have to make up your mind now, do you?' said Simon. 'Why don't you stay around for a few days anyway? You could pull the bus off the green. Put it in the garden of the cottage. Take a really good look at the place.'

'I don't know,' Max said. 'I'd need to take the stuff out of that shed. I'd need to see if it would make a studio.'

'I'm easy,' said Simon. 'Take your time. You know where to find me.'

'He's nice, isn't he?' said Rain, as they walked back to the bus.

'He wants to rent us a house,' replied Max. But then she smiled. 'Yeah, he seemed OK.'

In Max-speak, *OK* was pretty high on the

scale. The sun was setting behind the trees and the air was full of the sound of birds rustling and chattering as they settled down to sleep. *I have to ask her now*, Rain thought. *Now, while she's halfway cheerful.* 'I've been thinking,' she said. 'When we move into the cottage—'

'If,' said Max.

'All right, then, *if*. If we do, you'll be painting all day, won't you? What am I going to do?'

'The same as you've always done. Read. Make things. Gardening. There's plenty of that to do.'

'I'd be bored, Max. I'm not a kid any more, am I?' She hesitated. She knew Max would hate what she was going to say. But she had to say it. 'I want to go to school, Max.'

'School?' Max's face hardened. 'Yeah, right. I can just see you wearing a neat little uniform. Like those kids this afternoon. Get yourself brainwashed like the rest of them. You think they looked happy? You don't want that. Well? Do you?'

Rain had heard all this before of course, about ten million times. 'You twist everything, Max,' she said. Max made her so *angry* sometimes. 'I bet not all schools are like that. They can't be. And I *liked* those kids. Anyway, there are things I want to do with my life. And I won't be able to do them if I don't go to school.'

'Like what, exactly?'

'Like . . . like stopping them tearing up beautiful bits of countryside to build roads, for a start.'

'You don't have to go to school to do that. We can keep protesting. That's the way to stop them. Direct action.'

'So what good did protesting do?' demanded Rain. Last year they'd joined a big protest against a new road. There had been people living in tree-houses to stop the trees being felled and people living in tunnels to stop the diggers starting work. There had been others like themselves, travellers with vans and buses. And there had been local people, too: all kinds of people. It had felt great; it had seemed as if they were really doing something, but in the end, it had been useless. Rain knew she would never forget the sound of people screaming as the police dragged them away, or the sight of hundreds of uniformed men appearing out of the early morning mist. She shuddered.

'You've got your books,' Max said. 'You've got *me*.'

Rain didn't know what to say. Why did Max always have to make it *personal*? Max seemed to think you could learn everything from books, but it wasn't true. Sure, she'd learned plenty from books, but a lot of the most important things, she'd learned from people they'd met on the road, and from Max herself. Without Max, how could she have learned to read?

She thought about Crash, the hairy biker who had helped them out when the bus had broken down a couple of years before and they'd been stranded in a lay-by on a busy dual carriageway. He'd turned out to be the gentlest person Rain had ever met. Even Max hadn't managed to upset him. He'd also turned out to be a physics graduate, and Rain had talked to him for hours. He'd made studying physics sound like a fantastic adventure.

'You're right!' he'd said. 'That's exactly what it is. You should read about Feynman.' He'd rummaged in his bag and pulled out a small, dog-eared, oil-stained paperback. 'The man himself,' Crash told her. 'He wrote this. He made his whole life into an adventure. *And* he won the Nobel Prize.'

'You can't give me this,' Rain had said. 'It looks like you read it all the time.'

'I can get another one,' Crash had replied, and Rain had finally accepted the gift. She'd read the book from cover to cover several times, and one thing had become very clear to her as she'd read. Richard Feynman had made his life into an adventure, but the adventure had involved school, and exams, and university.

Max was still looking at her, waiting. 'I might want to go to university one day, Max,' she said. 'Can you teach me about quantum theory? Can you teach me to pass exams? You know you can't.'

Max was sullen and moody for days. She pulled all the junk out of the shed while Rain worked outside, slashing with the tools that Simon lent them at the ivy and brambles that covered the walls. Simon came over a couple of times during the week, but Max was so rude and silent that Rain was surprised he didn't simply tell them he'd decided he didn't want to rent them the cottage after all. She knew there was no point mentioning school again. She knew the signs. Max was building up to something.

It was five days before Max swept the last of the dust out of the door of the shed. Light streamed in through the windows Rain had cleaned. It was bigger than she'd expected. It would make a brilliant studio, and she could see Max thought so too.

'OK,' Max said. 'I've decided. This is the place. Everything feels right about it.' She looked at Rain. 'Well? Say something. You might look pleased.'

'There's no point in stopping though, is there?' Rain said. 'Not if I can't go to school.'

'OK, then.' Max turned her clear grey eyes on Rain. 'If that's really what you want, then you'd better do it. Only don't blame me if it all goes wrong.' Max paused. Then she said, 'When do you want to start?'

Rain felt as though she couldn't breathe. The sunshine was falling down through the leaves, and she watched it making patterns on the grass. She knew what Max was doing. She was calling her bluff. She'd never expected her to agree, not in a million years. She'd wanted to go school for so long, but now it came to the point, she was terrified. It was like standing on the side of one of the freezing river pools where she loved to swim. The longer you waited, the harder it was to jump. She took a deep breath.

'How about tomorrow?' she said.

3

Max didn't bother with formalities. She simply walked into the school and demanded to see the headteacher. Mrs Snowley was a small, round woman in a neat grey suit and Max looked tall and awkward beside her.

'We'll be very glad to have you, Rain,' the headteacher said. 'I'll get your mother to fill in some forms, and you can start on Monday.'

'But I want to start today,' Rain told her.

Max took the forms. 'I'll fill these in now. There's no reason why she can't start today, is there?'

'Well, there's the uniform, for a start.'

'I'll get it this afternoon. No problem.'

'I just think Rain might feel a little out of place in those clothes. It might be better to wait – until tomorrow at least.'

Rain looked down at her clothes. They were the most ordinary things she owned – a pair of jeans and a plain blue T-shirt. Maybe she should have worn the dress Grandma had given her last Christmas. But she *never* wore dresses. She would have felt stupid. Rain felt Max looking at her. 'I'll be fine,' she said. 'Honestly. I'd like to start today.'

'You see?' said Max. 'You take her where she needs to go and I'll stay here and fill in your forms.'

'Well . . .' Mrs Snowley began.

'Please,' said Rain.

'See you later, then,' Max said, picking up a pen and starting to write. 'I'll meet you after school.'

Mrs Snowley still looked worried, but she put a hand on Rain's shoulder and guided her into the corridor. 'I'll be back in ten minutes,' she told Max. 'I think we should talk.'

'Fine,' said Max. Rain felt tears pricking her eyes, and there was just a second when she nearly cracked. It was as if there were invisible wires that joined her to Max and she was cutting through one of them. She felt like running back and throwing her arms around her, but then Max looked up. 'Go on, then,' she said. 'What are you waiting for?' Rain turned and followed Mrs Snowley out of the room.

As they walked through the school Mrs

Snowley talked, but Rain didn't hear much of what she said. She was too busy looking around her, thinking how unreal it all seemed, worrying about what would happen next.

'. . . Mrs Haynes will be your class tutor. Registration with her, in your classroom, eight fifty-five prompt. And you'll need your uniform, of course.' She paused for a moment, glancing again at Rain's clothes. 'I'm afraid you won't be allowed to wear earrings either,' she said, looking at Rain's left ear, pierced by seven silver rings. 'You really don't *have* to start today, you know. I can talk to your mum.'

Rain shook her head. There was no going back now. 'I'll take the earrings out tonight,' she said.

Mrs Snowley started to say something else. Rain had the feeling she was about to ask her to take them out there and then, but she didn't. Instead, she moved on along the corridor. 'Here we are. Our destination. The art room.'

They stopped for a moment and Rain heard a man's voice. 'Sit down in your seats right now. You! Stephen Phillips, pick up that charcoal.'

Mrs Snowley opened the door, and the teacher's voice stopped suddenly.

'Trouble, Mr Hogan?'

'Nothing I can't deal with.' Mr Hogan had a grim smile on his face. The tips of his ears were crimson. A boy was scrabbling around among the feet of a group of children. Most of the others were grinning, but on the far side of the room Rain saw one face that wasn't even smiling. She recognized him straight away. It was Daniel, the boy from the garage. His face was pale and he looked exhausted. Rain saw a quick flicker of recognition in his eyes, then he looked down at his work again.

'Do that later, Stephen,' snapped Mrs Snowley. 'Sit down and keep still for a few moments, if that's possible. Now, you have a new member of your class. This is Rain Smith, everybody. I'm sure you'll make her very welcome. Charlene, perhaps you'll look after her this week, show her around.'

'Yes, Mrs Snowley.'

Rain wasn't sure she wanted to be looked after by Charlene, but she went and sat down in the empty chair while Mrs Snowley muttered to Mr Hogan. About her, presumably. She felt panic rising inside her. She told herself she'd been in scarier places than this, but she couldn't help it. She could feel them all looking at her. She could feel Charlene's eyes boring into her, and then she felt a sharp nudge in her side.

'Where you from, then?' Charlene whispered.

What could she say? There wasn't a simple answer, so Rain kept her mouth shut while Charlene continued to stare at her. She was glad when she saw the head-teacher coming towards them. 'Well now, girls,' Mrs Snowley said. 'Getting on all right? Good. I'm sure Charlene will take good care of you, Rain. I shall go and arrange things with your mother.'

The door clicked shut and Mr Hogan came over with a drawing board. 'I don't know how much you know about per-spective,' he said. 'Can't be less than some of these louts anyway. Have a go, OK?' He handed Rain a postcard with a picture of a city street on it. She nodded. Max had explained perspective to her plenty of times, but it hadn't made any difference. She couldn't draw for toffee. Still, at least she understood what she was meant to do. She began to work, and straight away she heard an uproar on the other side of the room.

'Sir! He jogged me, look!'

'Get out of it, Steve. Look what you've done.'

'Just leave it, Stephen, will you?' said Mr Hogan.

'I'm only doing what you said, sir, picking it up.'

'You can do it later. I'm warning you, Stephen, I've had about enough of this.'

As Stephen sat down, Rain caught Daniel's eye again, but he quickly looked away. He seemed very separate from the rest of them. They were all nudging each other and laughing as soon as the teacher had his back to them, but Daniel just kept his head down and worked. Rain picked up her pencil. Time passed. Charlene poked her again. 'Well?' she said.

'What?' Rain was starting to get annoyed, but she bit her lip and didn't say anything more.

'Where are you from? Are you thick or something?'

Luckily, before she could answer, she heard the teacher's voice. He was standing behind Daniel. 'What on earth are you doing, Daniel? What *is* this?' He reached down and picked up Daniel's paper. Daniel's face went bright red. He didn't speak.

'That's Daniel Moore,' Charlene whispered in Rain's ear. Her breath stank of cigarettes. 'He's pathetic.'

'I didn't mean to . . .' Daniel began. Mr Hogan stared at the drawing as if he was looking at a painting in a gallery. He held it away from him, then close up. Those nearby craned their necks, trying to see. Everyone had stopped working. Mr Hogan looked up from the drawing and he glanced straight at Rain. Then he looked back at the drawing again.

'This is good,' he said. 'It's not a perspective drawing of a city street, though, is it?' Daniel shook his head. 'Even so, it really is good. Take a look, everyone.'

He held the drawing up. Rain hardly heard all the stupid noises, the oohs and aahs. She felt herself blushing. The drawing was *her*. The crazy zig-zags of her spiky bleached blonde hair; an ear, with its seven earrings. She even recognized the tension that she could feel right now in her hunched shoulders. It was amazing.

'What made you do this?' Mr Hogan

asked. 'You've never done anything like it before.'

Daniel's face was deep crimson. There were more titters of laughter from around the room. 'Well, it really is a terrific drawing, Daniel,' Mr Hogan said, 'but now I think you'd better get back to what you *should* have been doing, OK? I'll fetch you some more paper.' He came back and patted Daniel on the shoulder. 'Well done,' he said.

'What a dork,' hissed Charlene. 'Looks like he's fallen in love.'

'You what?'

'Nothing.' Charlene pretended to get on with her work. Rain saw other people sneaking glances her way. She looked over at Daniel. She couldn't help herself. The drawing was astonishing. Why had he done it? More to the point, *how* had he done it? Rain would have given anything to be able to draw like that.

The bell went for the end of the lesson, and a group of boys gathered round Daniel, laughing and scuffling for a look at the picture. Daniel heaved his bag onto one shoulder and grabbed the paper. He pushed through the crowd, ripped the drawing in two, and chucked it in the bin. Then he hurried out of the door.

'They won't let you wear clothes like that,' said Marianne.

'And you're not allowed to wear earrings,' said a thin girl called Stacey.

'How'd you get that brown?' said one of the others. There were too many names to remember. Half a dozen girls, all asking questions. 'Is your dad a Paki? Only you don't look like a Paki, not really.'

After the art lesson Rain had been to PE, but she didn't have any kit, so she'd had to sit and watch. Now it was break time, and she'd had about enough of all these stupid questions, but there was no point making enemies, not on her first day. 'I'm getting a uniform. We didn't have time, that's all.'

'Where'd you go to school before, then? Didn't *they* have a uniform? You could have worn that, couldn't you? And I bet there aren't *any* schools that let you wear all those earrings.'

'I haven't been to school before,' Rain said.

They all stared at her. She could see they didn't believe her.

'Everyone goes to school.'

'Well, I didn't.'

'Why not?'

'I just didn't, that's all. I never wanted to. I didn't need to. My mum taught me.'

'I wouldn't want my mum teaching *me*,' laughed Stacey.

'Me neither,' said Charlene. 'Didn't they try and make you go to school? They do if you bunk off, don't they?'

'I . . . I don't know,' she said.

'What about your dad, then?' demanded Charlene.

'What do you mean?'

'Well, *he* must have tried to make you go.'

'I . . . my dad doesn't live with us.'

'Yeah, but don't you see him sometimes? I mean, when I nicked off school my dad was really angry with my mum for not stopping me, and he's got married again and got kids and everything.'

'Why do you keep going on about my dad? It's nothing to do with him. I've—' Rain stopped. She bit her lip. She felt angry and upset. She'd been on the point of blurting out the fact that she'd never even met her dad. She didn't know why she felt so upset. She knew she was making too much fuss.

'Just leave it, OK?' she said, looking around at the watching faces.

'We were only asking,' Stacey said. 'No need to get all huffy. You got some dark secret, have you?'

'Not in prison, is he?' Charlene asked, and they all laughed.

Rain knew she had to get away, but they were all around her. Then Stacey said, 'Hey, look! It's the great artist. Funny he drew you, Rain. Perhaps he fancies you?'

They all looked at Daniel. Rain shoved between them, and walked off across the playing field. There was a chain-link fence between her and the rest of the world. She watched the clouds moving slowly across the sky, waiting for her heart to slow down.

Somehow, she got through the rest of the day. She sat next to a different bunch of girls at lunch time. They asked just as many questions, but the questions didn't have the same kind of edge to them. One girl was tall, with long red hair and freckles. Her skirt was so short that Rain was sure it couldn't be legal. 'My name's Beth,' she said, 'and this is Alice.'

The other girl was dark and quiet, but she smiled at Rain. 'Is it right what the others say, that you live in a bus and you've never been to school?'

'Yes.'

'Did you go to festivals and stuff?' asked Beth. 'Glastonbury, places like that?'

'We went to Glastonbury once,' Rain said. 'We hated it though. Too many people. Why? Have you been?'

'You must be joking. Our mums and dads would never take us anywhere like that. Would they, Alice?' Alice shook her head. 'You're dead lucky. Tell us what it was like. When did you go? What bands did you see?'

Rain told them about the worst festival she'd ever been to, every detail: the mud, the loos, the rip-offs. They didn't listen, though.

'Must have been great,' Beth said, dreamily. 'You must be completely crazy to want to give all that up for this.'

When school finished, Rain wasn't sure what to do. It was only four o'clock, and Max had said she'd meet her at 4.15. Tomorrow she was going to have to catch the school bus. She watched them all fighting their way on, and she was glad she didn't have to do it tonight. She was sick of people asking her questions. She noticed Daniel, hanging back behind the others. He'd been in her class for most of the lessons she'd had today. She remembered the drawing. Had it really been that good? Maybe if she went back to the art room . . . She looked at her watch. There was plenty of time.

Mr Hogan was pottering around, tidying up, when Rain opened the door. He smiled when he saw her.

'Hi there. Rain, isn't it? Had a good first day, then? What can I do for you?'

'Could I have that drawing?' Rain said. 'I mean, you'll only chuck it away, won't you?'

He looked puzzled. 'It was only an exercise, you know. And I generally keep them till the end of term. Still, if it'll make you happy . . .' He began leafing through a pile of drawings of London streets.

'No. I mean the one Daniel did. The drawing of me. The one he ripped up and threw away.'

'Good Lord. I'd forgotten all about that. An uncharacteristic flash of genius from young Daniel. I don't see why you shouldn't have it if you can find it. It is *you* after all.'

Rain searched through the bin and found the pieces of paper. She smoothed them out on a table and fitted them together. 'Here,' Mr Hogan said. He handed her a roll of tape. He looked at the drawing for a moment. 'A one-off, most likely,' he said. 'Never see him do that again, poor kid.'

Rain almost asked him what he meant. It seemed an odd thing for a teacher to say. But Mr Hogan was already busy again with his marking. She folded the paper carefully and put it in her bag. Max was waiting for her when she reached the gate.

'Good day?' she said.

'Sure. Why wouldn't it be? How are we getting back?' Simon had brought them into town that morning, but there was no sign of him now.

'Over there,' said Max. Rain looked where she was pointing. On the far side of the road was a rusting white van. 'It's big enough to sleep in when we go away,' said Max. 'And I can fit my canvases inside.'

Rain couldn't believe it. Max had gone out and bought a van without taking her along. They'd always done everything together. Max started the engine, and Rain lifted the bonnet. 'What do you think?' asked Max.

'You're crazy,' said Rain. 'I mean, look at the engine. I reckon the cylinder head gasket's leaking.' She pulled the dipstick from the engine. 'See? Look at the state of the oil. Didn't you check?'

'You were at school. And I was in a hurry. I had your school uniform to buy. Anyway, Simon looked at it. He reckoned it was a bargain, and there's nothing that can't be fixed, he says. Maybe you could fix it?'

'Maybe,' said Rain.

When they arrived home, Rain helped Max unload the bags from the back of the van. Most of them seemed to be full of school clothes. 'Here,' said Max. 'Try them on while I cook the tea.'

Rain carried the clothes into the bus and dumped them on her bed. She'd never really had any new clothes before, apart from underwear and socks, and the dresses Grandma sent her every Christmas, which she never wore. Her clothes had always come from jumble sales or charity shops. Even the jumpers Max had knitted for her when she was little had been knitted from wool unravelled from old jumble sale jumpers. These school clothes were stiff, and they smelt funny. They lay on top of her patchwork quilt like a dark pool. As she stared at them, she heard words in her head. *'What about your dad, then?'*

Suddenly she felt as if everything was going wrong. Everything was changing. Not having a dad had never bothered her before. She remembered asking Max about him once, when she was still quite little. Max had shown her a strip of photos, the ones you got from a machine. She'd told Rain they didn't need him, they were fine on their own, the two of them, and that had been enough for Rain. It was just those stupid girls at school . . .

She picked up a black sweatshirt. She felt scared. She could stop it all if she wanted. I don't *have* to do it, she told herself. I don't *have* to go to school. And if I tell Max I've gone off the idea of living here, I bet she'll change her mind.

But then she saw the book lying open on her bed. It was called *Chaos*. She'd seen a review of it in the back of the book Crash had given her, and she'd managed to persuade Max to stop the bus on the edge of Glasgow one day in June while she'd caught the train into the city and bought the book.

It was full of amazing ideas, and Rain had spent hours puzzling over them, but there was still too much that she didn't understand, complicated ideas to do with mathematics and science. Max couldn't explain them to her. She knew because she'd asked her.

'Maths!' Max had said. 'You know I can't do maths. Why bother with that?' As if there was something wrong with being interested in maths. If Rain had been good at music or painting, that would have been different, of course. She *had* to go to school, whatever Max thought, however hard it turned out to be. She'd handled a lot worse things in her life than a few stupid girls.

She began to try on the black clothes.

Rain woke early the next morning, but not nearly as early as Max. She looked out of the window of the bus and saw Max sitting on a log by the fire with a drawing board across her knees. Rain wrapped herself in an old coat and went outside. Max saw her and put a finger to her lips. Rain stared into the bushes, trying to see what she was drawing. The sun was just coming up through layers of mist, and every bush was covered in dew. Then she noticed the splash of red.

A fox was sitting on the far side of the clearing. It was dead still. A ray of sunlight came through the bushes and lit up the hairs on its back. They were brilliant orange. They glowed. Rain saw Max's hand blur across the paper and then, all at once, the fox was gone. It simply melted away into the undergrowth.

'Can I see?' Rain asked. Max passed her the board. At first, all she could see were meaningless lines, but she was used to looking at Max's drawings. The marks suddenly seemed to rearrange themselves. The fox was alive on the paper. 'It's amazing,' she said. Then she remembered Daniel's picture.

'I want to show you something,' she said. She took the drawing out of her bag and spread it on the drawing board.

Max stared at it. 'You never did this? Why is it ripped?'

Rain explained about Daniel. 'What a waste,' said Max. 'That's school for you. You'd better get your uniform on. The bus will be here at eight-o-three, that's what they told me. It sounds like a military operation.'

'You agreed,' Rain said, turning to go indoors. 'It's what I want. You know that.'

Max was still drawing in the garden when she came back outside. She felt as if she was wearing someone else's clothes.

'You've taken your earrings out,' said Max.

'Not all of them. I kept this one in, look. The first one.' Max had bought the tiny sapphire for her when she was five, for her birthday. It was her first ever earring.

'They'll make you take it out,' Max said.

'They won't. It's tiny. They won't even notice.'

Then she had to run to catch the bus.

When she got home that night Max was painting the kitchen. 'I'm going to paint the whole house white,' she said. There were five enormous tins of paint by the door.

'I'll help,' said Rain. 'Just let me change.' She couldn't wait to get out of the uniform. She was already beginning to see what school was going to be like. Every chance they got, Charlene and her friends made some stupid comment, or asked a daft question. She would never have believed how annoying it could be.

'Wait,' Max said. 'I've got to go into town to see a solicitor. He's not quite as cool about the whole deal as Simon is. You'd better come with me.'

The solicitor's office was right opposite the school. On the playing field across the road a bunch of boys were playing football. There was a kids' playground there too, where a couple of little girls were playing on the swings. 'Hiya!' yelled the biggest one. 'It's me, Kerry.'

'I'll wait over there,' Rain said to Max. 'OK?'

Max nodded and walked across the road. Rain had a vague idea that you were supposed to dress up a bit when you went to see a solicitor. Max was wearing a tie-dyed vest and a pair of cut-off jeans. She had put some shoes on, though. Rain smiled when she saw that. Maybe Max *had* dressed up after all.

'Watch me,' Kerry yelled to her. 'I can swing really high without anyone pushing.'

'Where's your mum and dad, then?' Rain asked her. There didn't seem to be anyone with them.

'Mum's at work,' Annette said.

'Again,' added Kerry.

'She's always at work,' Annette agreed.

'So when Dad brings Daniel to football, we have to come. We hate football. Dad's over there, watching Daniel.'

Rain could see Tony, standing by the side of the pitch. Hayley was running up and down in the mud nearby.

'She'll be completely covered in it by the time we go home,' said Kerry.

'She always is,' said Annette. 'She likes it.'

'Daniel doesn't,' said Kerry.

You didn't have to be a genius to see that, thought Rain. She walked closer, curious to see what was going on. Daniel was standing on his own on the far side of the field. A small man in glasses and tracksuit was running up and down, screaming at the boys. 'Drop off round the back, son! Pull over! Pull over! Pick one of them up! Get stuck in!'

It sounded like rubbish to Rain. It didn't look as if the boys understood it either. She recognized quite a few of them from school. Stephen was there, and Darren. Then someone yelled and fell over and the game stopped. Daniel looked in her direction, so she waved. He didn't wave back. His shirt had writing on, big letters saying, MOORE'S MOTOR SERVICES. Several of the others were wearing them, too. Then she heard Tony shout. 'Wake up, Daniel, for crying out loud! Pick someone up! Get yourself into the game.'

Daniel shrugged, and turned away. Rain could see just by looking at him that he hated the whole thing. So why was he doing it? She looked at Tony. His fists were clenched tightly at his side, his eyes riveted to the game. Something wet and muddy crashed into Rain's legs. She yelped, and Tony turned round.

'Hayley! What have you done now?' Hayley was sitting by Rain's feet in the mud. She started to cry. Tony went to pick her up, and then he recognized Rain. 'Oh,' he said, 'it's you. Girl mechanic. What are you doing here? I thought you'd be miles away by now.' He wiped the mud off Hayley's face. She was staring at Rain.

'Where's your bus?' she demanded suddenly.

'It's at home,' said Rain.

Tony looked a question at her. 'We found somewhere to live,' she said. 'A house. Not far from you. I'm going to Daniel's school. I thought he would have said.'

Hayley slipped her muddy hand into Rain's and started pulling her towards the swings. 'Good with kids, aren't you?' Tony said, as he walked beside them.

'I like them, that's all.'

'No brothers and sisters then?' She shook her head. Questions, always questions. 'And you've, like, always lived in that bus?'

'I was born in it.'

'Must have been quite a shock, then, when it broke down?'

'You can say that again.' Rain was surprised. It seemed almost as if he understood. She was about to ask him about his garage, and the name on the shirts, when she heard the van. Max was honking the horn. Even from where they were standing the engine sounded like a load of scrap metal going round in a washing machine.

'That yours? It's a bit rough, isn't it?'

Before Rain could reply Daniel walked past them without saying a word. Tony went after him, talking the whole time. 'Everyone has off days,' Rain heard him say. 'You just need to do a bit more work on technique. We can do it at the weekend. What you need to do is this . . .'

His voice faded as they walked away. Max hooted again. Rain said goodbye to the girls and ran to the van.

'Isn't that that boy?' Max asked. 'The one who did the drawing?'

'Daniel,' said Rain. She looked across the road and saw Daniel and his dad facing each other on the small car park. Daniel was shouting angrily at his dad as the three girls got into the back of the car.

Max drove along a lane that skirted the far side of the playing field. Rain could see the roofs of the school in the distance. 'Where are you going?' she asked. 'This isn't the way home.'

'I was looking at the map,' said Max. 'Just along here there are marshes, and a river. Look.'

She stopped the van on the verge. The land dropped away sharply. A wide green expanse began just below them and stretched away as far as they could see. Winding through the green water meadows Rain saw the line of trees that marked where the river ran, and beyond that, miles away and very small, the flash of sunlight on the houses of a village. 'That'll be where the sea is,' said Max, pointing into the distance beyond the stubby black shapes of old windmills where the marsh faded into mist.

They got out of the van and Rain stood there, feeling the cold, clean wind on her face. 'This is what I'm going to paint,' said Max. 'As soon as we've moved into the cottage, this'll be the very first thing I do.'

That night, Rain had a dream. She was in the bus. Through the windscreen she could see grey sea, and mist, and the shapes of

floating islands. She turned to say something to Max, but Max wasn't there. The
man in the driver's seat was wearing some
kind of hat, and he was looking away from
her. But it was her dad. She knew it was.
He started to turn towards her. Any second
she would see his face . . .

Rain woke with a jolt. She was shivering,
and she couldn't work out where she was for
a moment. Moonlight was shining in
through the window of the bus. She looked
around at the familiar shapes. Soon, they'd
be moving out. For so long it had just been
her and Max, but now it was all changing.
She couldn't shake the memory of the
dream. She wanted to see her dad's face,
but she was scared, too. She drifted back to
sleep, but when she woke up the dream was
still with her.

The morning was fine, almost like summer
now the October mist was lifting, and Max
was sitting outside by the fire, eating her
muesli. It was almost as if they were still on
the road. The old black kettle was bubbling,
so Rain made some tea. She looked at
Max. 'I had a dream,' she said. Max was
interested in dreams. She was always

trying to work out what they meant.

'What kind of a dream? Good? Bad? Nightmare?'

'It . . . It was about my dad.'

'Yeah?' said Max. She put her bowl down on a log. 'What's brought this on, then?'

'Why don't you ever talk about him?'

'I never even think about him. You haven't asked about him for years.'

'People keep asking me. And I was thinking about Daniel and his family. I just started thinking what it was like, having a dad. And then I had this dream.'

'Did you see him, then, in your dream?'

Rain shook her head. 'We were in the bus. I couldn't see his face. What was he like, Max?'

'He was a laugh, I suppose, at first. But then he changed.'

'You . . . you sound like you didn't like him.'

'Oh, I liked him all right. But I went off him pretty quick. If he'd had *his* way we'd have got married and bought a nice little house. He was like a different person once he knew *you* were on the way. So I told him to forget it. I didn't need him.'

'But what did he look like? What was he called?'

'His name was Cameron,' Max said. She was looking into the fire. 'He was tall, like me. Brown eyes. What else can I tell you? It was a long time ago. We were at art school together. I haven't seen him since the day I drove off in the bus.'

A blackbird flew onto the roof of the cottage and started singing. 'There's a picture, isn't there?' said Rain. 'I saw it once, I'm sure I did.'

'Maybe. Somewhere.' Max looked at her sharply. 'You *are* enjoying school? It's going OK?'

'Of course I am,' Rain said. 'And anyway, I've only just started. What's that got to do with my dad?'

'Nothing,' said Max. She stood up and stretched. 'Come on, then. Let's rake through the past.'

She made her way to the back of the bus and started pulling boxes from the cupboard underneath her bed. Right at the back she found an old biscuit tin with a picture of an ocean liner on the lid. Hundreds of letters and photographs spilled out as she opened it.

Rain saw the small strip of photos, and immediately she *knew*. She felt hot and cold at the same time. Two heads were crammed into the pictures, laughing and pulling faces. 'That's him,' she said. 'Isn't it?'

Max took the pictures from her hand. She looked at them for a moment, and then she handed them back. 'Sure,' she said. 'That's him.'

Rain walked slowly back down the bus, staring at the tiny images. He looked like a boy. He didn't look much older than she was. He was blurred, out of focus. He was pulling a stupid face. He could have been anyone. But she heard Max's words in her head. *He was like a different person when he knew you were on the way*. He'd cared about her, even if he'd never known her.

'I'd tell you more if I could,' said Max. 'But that's all there is. And haven't you got a timetable to stick to?'

Rain looked at her watch. She had six minutes before the bus arrived. She stuffed the strip of photos under her pillow, grabbed her things, and ran.

Rain did her best to keep out of the way of Charlene and Stacey at school. She stuck with Beth and Alice, which was OK, but they'd been best mates since they were about four, and there wasn't really room for anyone else. Not that they weren't friendly, but once Rain had finished describing every festival she'd ever been to, they didn't have that much to talk about. Mostly, they seemed to talk about programmes they'd seen on TV, and as Rain didn't *have* a TV, that made conversation difficult.

There seemed to be school rules about absolutely everything. One afternoon in the second week a man in a suit with a clipboard made of imitation crocodile skin stopped Rain in the corridor. 'Look at your shirt,' he said.

Rain looked. 'What's wrong?' she asked.

'You know what's wrong.'

'No, I don't.'

'Don't make it worse for yourself by being cheeky.'

'But . . .'

'Sir, she's new.' Rain looked round and saw Daniel. The man gave him a dirty look. 'It's true, sir. She started last week.'

'Right, then. I'll tell you once. I am Mr Crawley and I am the deputy headteacher with special responsibility for uniform. Pupils at this school keep their shirts neatly tucked in. Shirt hanging out like that –' he pointed at Rain's – 'equals detention. Understood?'

He strutted off down the corridor. 'Thanks,' Rain said to Daniel. 'He thinks he's really something, doesn't he?'

Daniel looked embarrassed. 'It's OK,' he said. 'You have to watch out for the Creep. You're lucky he didn't spot that earring.' Rain's hand flew up to her ear. 'It just, you know, caught the light,' Daniel said. 'And you should call him *sir*,' he went on, looking even more embarrassed.

'How are your sisters?'

'My sisters? Oh, right, you were playing with them. They're the same as usual.'

There were loads of things Rain wanted to ask him about – about his dad, about why he played football when he obviously hated it, about the drawing – only she didn't know how to start. 'I'll see you around, then,' Daniel said finally.

'Yeah, right,' said Rain. 'See you.'

'Ooh, look,' said Stacey's voice from further down the corridor. 'Together again.'

Daniel flushed and walked quickly away.

Another week went by. Max painted and painted. The inside of the cottage turned slowly white. It looked amazing, full of light, but Rain could see that Max was itching to get it all finished and start doing *real* painting again. And she hated Rain doing homework, especially when she thought Rain should be helping her.

'They've got hours every day to teach you all this stuff,' she said one evening, picking up Rain's maths book and flicking through the pages. 'Why do they need to make you do more at night?'

They were sitting in the bus. Max had a sketchbook on her lap as usual, her tongue sticking out as she drew. With every day that went by Rain had the feeling that something was slipping away from her. The bus was a part of her, like a second skin, like the shell of a snail. She knew every centimetre of it so well – the splash of yellow on the floor where Max had spilt a tin of paint and they'd decided to leave it because it looked so good, and the tiny luminous stars that Max had painted on the roof so that, in winter, they'd feel as if they were sleeping under the night sky. In the summer they slept outside under the stars as often as they possibly could.

'Go on, then,' said Max. 'Tell me. What's the point of homework?'

'If you keep asking stupid questions, I'll never finish it,' said Rain, who was wondering herself what the point was of doing thirty sums that she already knew how to do. 'And then I'll get a detention . . . I think.' In fact, she wasn't sure about that either, because it seemed to depend on the teacher. It was all very tricky. 'What are you drawing?' she asked.

Max turned the book towards her and she saw herself, tongue sticking out, book in hand, frowning horribly. 'Max! I don't look like that.'

'It's the effect of the homework,' said Max. She stood up. 'I'm going to do some more work in the cottage. See you in the morning.'

When she'd finished her homework, Rain curled up on her bed and tried to read, but she found that her mind kept drifting back to school. She wished she could talk to Max about it. It wasn't just the homework and the rules that were stupid. Other things annoyed her, too. For a start, it seemed as if every time a lesson started to get interesting, the bell rang. It had happened again today. They'd had a lesson in the computer room about using the Internet. She'd been nervous at first, but she couldn't believe how simple it was to use a search engine. You could just type in a word, any word, and click a button. She'd typed Feynman, and a whole list of web pages had appeared. She'd clicked on one and a picture of Richard Feynman himself had appeared on the screen. She'd started reading. She was still reading when the bell went. 'That's it then,' the teacher had said, over the clattering of chairs. 'Off you go.'

'But I've only just started,' Rain had said, before she could stop herself. 'I can carry on next time, can't I?'

'Next week is data handling. Look, I'm sorry,' the teacher had told her. 'I have to cover the curriculum, you know. Why don't you come to computer club? Thursday lunch times.'

It was late when Rain closed her book, but she could still see Max's silhouette in the lighted window of the cottage, painting away. She yawned, and then pulled the strip of photos from under her pillow. She fell asleep looking at the grinning stranger, wondering where he was now.

The week after that, Rain got to see inside the metalwork shop, but it turned out they weren't going to do metalwork at all. Instead, they did something that her timetable called Design and Technology. They made key rings out of pieces of plastic. The teacher looked as if he was bored to death.

'Well done,' he said, when he glanced at Rain's key ring at the end of the lesson. He'd said that to everyone.

'Sir?' asked Rain. 'When do we get to do metalwork? You know, use the lathes and everything?'

The teacher laughed. 'You're new around here, aren't you?' he said. 'Nice to see a bit of enthusiasm, though.' He crossed to the wall and took down a fat folder. 'Ah, here we are. Term three. You get to make a steel shelf bracket. Correction, you design it, then you make it. OK?'

'But what about the forge?' said Rain. 'And all those machine tools. There's enough stuff here to . . . to make a car or something.'

She heard some of the others starting to laugh, but she didn't care. She wanted to know. But the teacher had lost interest. 'Shelf brackets,' he repeated. 'Term three. Now clear off, you lot. That's the bell, thank God.'

Maths wasn't hard, and neither was science. In fact, both subjects were disappointingly easy. Even though Max wasn't interested in science, they'd met several people on the road who were. Rain smiled when she thought about some of the people she'd learned things from. There was an old Scottish crofter who'd been a navigator in the RAF. He was great at geometry and arithmetic. And the landlady of a pub in a village where they'd spent a few weeks had been a chemist in a big food company before she'd retired. She'd almost managed to convince Rain that chemistry was the most important science of all.

Some lessons were harder. German was tough because Rain had never done any, but when she heard Charlene talking she couldn't believe she'd been learning it for over a year. And then there was English.

'We're going to carry on reading *Handles*,' Mrs Haynes told them. 'Perhaps one of you would like to tell Rain what has happened so far? Natalie?'

The book sounded interesting, about a girl who loved motorbikes and went to stay with some weird relations in the country. It sounded like it could really have happened. It even had places Rain knew in it, like Norwich. 'Thank you, Natalie,' said Mrs Haynes. 'Now, we'll take it in turns to read a little. Off you go, Roy.'

For a few seconds, Rain started to worry about having to read in front of all these other people. The feeling lasted as long as the first two sentences of Roy's reading. He read incredibly slowly, one word at a time. Someone else took over, reading faster, sounding like a machine gun, belting out the words, ignoring the full stops. It was almost impossible to understand. Rain stopped listening. It was too painful. She skimmed on down the page and turned over . . .

'Rain!' Mrs Haynes's voice jerked her back to reality. 'Would you like to have a try?'

'Yeah, sure,' Rain said without thinking. 'Where did you get to?'

There were a few snorts of laughter. The girl next to her pointed to the place, and she began to read. She read the way she sometimes read to Max, when she was painting and she'd found a really good bit she wanted to read to her. She forgot she was in a classroom, and Mrs Haynes didn't stop her. She read on, page after page, to the end of the chapter.

When she finished there was silence. Either they'd all been listening, or they'd fallen asleep. A boy's voice broke the stillness. It was Stephen. 'What a dweeb,' he said.

They all laughed. Rain felt herself going red. Then she thought, *Why should I feel embarrassed. This is stupid.* And she started to feel angry.

'Quiet, everyone,' Mrs Haynes said. 'Thank you very much, Rain. That was terrific. A real pleasure.'

Rain heard Charlene's voice next to her, mocking. 'Thank you, Rain. A real pleasure.'

'You, Stephen,' Mrs Haynes snapped, 'you

can read next, and then you, Wayne. And you needn't think I haven't noticed your behaviour.'

Stephen started reading. He could read all right, but he made it sound as if he hated every word. He was making a point. His reading was directed at Rain. Each word was like a bullet. He was telling her this was how you did it; this was the cool way. 'Now then, Wayne,' said Mrs Haynes.

Wayne read like a robot. His voice was flat and dull. Rain listened for a few moments, and then began to read to herself again. Before she knew it, the lesson was over. 'Just stay behind a moment, will you, Rain?' said Mrs Haynes.

'Teacher's pet, that's what you're going to be,' said Charlene, picking up her bag.

Mrs Haynes sighed, and waited until the rest of the class had finished making their noisy exit. Rain saw that, like most of the teachers, she looked very tired. 'I thought you might like to borrow these.' She handed Rain some books. 'They're by the same author. You obviously like her stuff.'

'Thanks. That's brilliant. Are you sure it's OK?'

'Well, you read half of that one during the

lesson, so you're going to need something else to read, aren't you?'

'Sorry,' said Rain. 'I mean, thanks.'

'No trouble,' said Mrs Haynes. 'How are you settling in? How are you finding school?'

'It's . . . It's OK.'

Mrs Haynes looked at her. 'Well, good. Enjoy the books.'

Rain shut the door behind her.

'That was *lovely* reading, Rain,' said Stephen's voice.

'*Terrific* reading,' said Wayne.

'Why don't you read a bit more, just for us,' said Charlene.

'We'd really love you to. It sounds so *lovely* when you read, Rain,' said Stacey.

Rain stared at them.

'Yeah, get your book out,' said Stephen, laughing. 'Here, give us your bag and I'll get it out for you.' He tried to grab the bag from her shoulder. She pulled back and the shoulder strap broke. Pencils and books clattered onto the floor.

Rain saw red. In her head she heard the crash of a brick through the window of the bus, she saw Max standing in the doorway, silhouetted in the headlights, screaming as tyres squealed and a car roared away.

'Pick them up,' she hissed. Her face was white. 'Go on. Do it.'

Stephen hesitated. Then Stacey said, 'My dad says people like you and your mum are just the same as gippos. He says you shouldn't be allowed to live in buses and vans. He says—'

Rain stepped towards her as the classroom door opened and Mrs Haynes appeared.

'What's going on?' she demanded. 'Rain, what are you doing?'

Rain was suddenly aware of her clenched fists. Her fingernails were biting into her palms. 'Nothing,' she said. She saw a little smile flicker across Stacey's face. 'I dropped my bag, that's all.' She bent to pick up the things, and hurried off along the corridor, blinking back her tears.

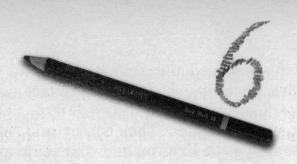

The following day Rain saw Daniel trapped in a corner of the playground by a small group of boys. She moved closer to see what was going on.

'You going to be there on Sunday, then?' Stephen was saying. 'Or have you got to stay at home and look after your sisters?'

'Or maybe his car'll break down again,' said Darren. 'Funny, isn't it, how your car keeps breaking down when your dad's meant to be a mechanic.'

'That's why he went bust,' Stephen said. 'He's useless. My dad says he couldn't fix an egg whisk.'

'He's not useless,' Daniel said angrily.

Rain pushed between two of the boys and stood in front of him. 'I've been looking for you,' she said. She turned round and stared at the others. 'Yeah?' she demanded. 'What are you waiting for? You want something? Come on, Daniel, let's go.'

Stephen moved to stand in her way but

she didn't hesitate. She hadn't been ready for them the day before. She hadn't been expecting it. But this was different. She put a hand on Stephen's shoulder and shoved him steadily backwards, enjoying the confusion on his face. She heard his mates giggling at him as she walked past them. Daniel followed her down the corridor.

'You shouldn't have done that,' he said. 'You'll just make it worse.'

'Oh yeah? How, exactly?'

'You don't want to make Stephen into an enemy. Take my word for it.'

'I've already done that, haven't I? What have you done to upset them so much? Why do they pick on you like that? Why do you let them?'

'You think it's that easy? What am I supposed to do?'

'Can't you tell a teacher?'

Daniel just looked at her. 'What do you think a teacher would do? There'd be a big inquisition. They'd ask for both sides of the story, and *if* they believed me they *might* give Stephen and his mates a bit of a telling off. And after that they'd be worse than ever. So, no thanks, I'll deal with it myself.'

It didn't look to Rain as if Daniel was

dealing with anything. 'But . . . you play football with them, don't you? I saw you.'

Daniel was silent. Then he said, 'I'm rubbish at football. I only play because Dad . . . he sponsored the team . . . you must have seen the shirts. And that's a joke too, because there isn't a Moore's Motor Services any more, is there? I wouldn't even be in the team if Dad hadn't done that. They'd have dropped me ages ago.'

'But you don't have to play, do you? Not if you don't want to.'

'It's what Dad wants,' Daniel said.

Rain stared at him. It was as if he didn't have a mind of his own, as if he didn't have any control over anything, as if he'd given up. But it was Daniel who'd done that amazing drawing, who had a talent that she would have given almost anything to possess. 'But you can draw,' she said. The words jerked out of her involuntarily. To her astonishment, she saw Daniel blushing.

'No, I can't,' he said. 'That . . . that was an accident. I don't know how I did it. It was rubbish.'

'It was good,' Rain said. 'You know it was. I know it was. My mum's a painter. Believe me, *I* know.'

'You don't know anything,' said Daniel. 'So leave me alone, OK?'

Rain watched him go. He was easy to upset, that was for sure. Moody, miserable. But even though he looked like the rest of them, she was sure he was an outsider, the same as her.

Saturday morning came, and Rain slept late. She still couldn't believe how tired it made her feel, going to school every day. When she looked out of the window she saw Max and Simon walking towards the cottage carrying the gas stove between them. Max had started moving into the cottage without her. She jumped out of bed and ran to the door of the bus. 'You should have waited for me,' she yelled.

Max put her end of the cooker down on the grass. She was laughing at something Simon had said. 'I tried to wake you up,' she called back. 'You would have slept through an earthquake.'

Rain yawned and looked around. All the pots and pans were gone, all the plates and cups, the cooker, the fridge. Only patches of dust and grease were left behind. It was real. It was happening. They were actually moving out. She realized now that a part of her had always felt that as long as they were still in the bus, they might move on again. They still had wheels underneath them. But now . . .

'What's the matter?' asked Max. 'Don't look so miserable.'

'It's the bus,' Rain said. 'It's our home. I feel like I'm leaving our home behind. The house is . . . well, it's just a house, isn't it?'

'It's going to be good,' Max said. 'You'll see. We're like hermit crabs. This shell's too small for us. We need a bigger one.'

'It hasn't got wheels though, has it?'

'We've got the van,' Max said. 'When you've fixed it we'll be able to go away whenever we feel like it. I thought this was what you wanted.'

Rain felt a wave of guilt. She'd always done small jobs on the bus, jobs they didn't need to pay a garage for. And maybe if she tried she *could* get the van running properly. Only – it wasn't the bus, it wasn't her *home*, and anyway, there'd been homework, and helping with the painting . . . 'I haven't had time,' she said.

'I know,' said Max. 'I wasn't hassling you. Not about that, anyway. But you are going to help with the moving, aren't you? It'll seem much more like home when you've got all your things in your room.'

It didn't take very long to move all their belongings. The bus had seemed full of stuff, but once it was inside the cottage, it didn't seem like very much at all. Rain and Max each had a mattress, a box of clothes and a stack of books, but they had no furniture at all apart from the camping table and folding chairs that were standing outside by the fire. The tables in the bus were flaps of wood that folded down from the walls when they were needed, but they were no use in the house. They took the two old bus seats, the only remaining original ones, into the front room of the cottage to make a sofa.

'That's it, then,' said Max, 'apart from what's going in the studio, but I've got to make some shelves before I move in there.'

'It's a bit bare, isn't it?' said Simon, looking around doubtfully. 'I'm sure I've got some furniture I could lend you. The house is full of bits and pieces Mum and Dad collected over the years. You can hardly move in some of the rooms. And you could do with a rug or two, couldn't you?'

Rain waited for Max to bite his head off. Nobody told Max what she needed. Nobody really ever got close to Max. But Max was smiling. 'I like it bare,' she said. She spun round with her arms outstretched. 'It's great to have space. It's great to be able to move without knocking something over. But I guess it would be good to have one or two chairs.'

'Only thing is, you'll have to pay me back,' Simon said. He was smiling too. 'I've got heaps and heaps of muck in the yard. It all needs carting away.'

'Come on then,' said Max. 'Let's take a look. You coming, Rain?'

Simon made them some sandwiches for lunch and then they went outside into the yard. This was the first chance Rain had had to have a proper look at the farm. If the house was crooked and old, the barns and sheds were even more so. 'It looks like the little crooked man ought to live here,' she said.

'Yeah, well,' Simon grinned, 'Dad was a bit like that. That's why the fields are crooked too. But it all got a bit out of hand before he died.'

The barns and sheds surrounded an

overgrown grassy area. There were several mysterious-looking heaps covered with stinging nettles.

'Dad kept a few cows and pigs,' said Simon. 'Right to the end. He was eighty, you know. He just keeled over one day with a heart attack while he was feeding them.'

'I'm sorry,' said Max.

'Don't be,' said Simon. 'It's the way he would have wanted to go. The pigs and cows were sold when he died, but there's all their . . . well, you know . . . muck . . . left behind. These heaps, and more in the sheds. It all needs shovelling out. What do you think? It's all organic, mind. Dad never used a chemical in his life.'

Max grabbed a fork and started work, shovelling crumbly brown stuff into a barrow. Rain was surprised to find that it hardly smelt at all, just a musty, old smell, and she enjoyed working beside Max in the half darkness of the barn under the old wooden beams – they were crooked too, she noticed. They filled barrow after barrow, wheeling them out into the yard, making a new heap beside all the others, but after she'd been working for an hour or so, Rain felt her hands getting sore. She went outside to look, and saw two big blisters on her palm.

Simon jumped down from the tractor. 'Come inside,' he said. 'I'll put something on them for you.'

The kitchen hadn't changed, and the computer was still sitting on the table. 'You want a go?' said Simon, placing a dressing on her hand. 'I should have realized your hands wouldn't cope with that sort of work.'

'Does this connect to the Internet?' asked Rain.

'Sure,' said Simon. 'Just click there. Disconnect when you're done, OK?'

Rain had been to the computer club at school the week before. She'd been surprised to find that she was the only girl there, but that hadn't bothered her. From the moment she had logged on she had been in another world, moving from website to website, amazed at how much there was, how easy it was. When the bell had gone for the end of lunch time she'd realized she hadn't even eaten her lunch. She'd had to run to avoid being late for her next lesson.

Now, on Simon's computer, she had all the time she wanted, but for some reason she just couldn't get going. She found herself gazing around the kitchen, looking at the titles on the spines of the books on the shelves, wondering about Simon, wondering why it was that Max seemed to get on with him when she'd hardly got on with anyone for as far back as Rain could remember.

Leaf came and put his head on her lap. Rain stroked him, and then winced as she felt the pain from her blisters. She looked at her hands. When they'd been on the road her hands had been tough. Even a few weeks ago she'd done all that work in the garden, but since starting school she'd hardly done anything like that. Then she heard Max and Simon laughing outside and knew she couldn't sit in here all day listening to them. She thought suddenly of Daniel and his sisters. Their house wasn't far, not if she took the old bike that was still strapped to the back of the bus. She disconnected from the Internet and went outside.

Max rested on her fork, sweating and smiling as Rain told her where she was going. 'That's a good idea,' she said. 'If I'm not at home when you get back, then I'll be here.'

As Rain walked away she felt a twist in her stomach. Max and Simon were friendly. That was OK. But what if it was more than that? What then?

You couldn't miss Daniel's house. It was only a hundred metres from the garage. Rain had seen it from the school bus, a big square red brick building with an untidy spread of uncut grass in front of it. Brightly coloured children's toys were dotted about in the grass – two small pink bikes, a doll's buggy on its side with a giant teddy still strapped in, a wheelbarrow full of plastic bricks. As she stood outside, straddling her bike and wondering if there was anyone home, Tony's rusty blue car pulled into the driveway.

'Hi,' Rain began. 'I've come to see Daniel. Is he . . . ?'

She wasn't sure if Tony had even heard her. He rushed into the house, leaving the front door open. She heard him calling. 'Dan? Kerry, Hayley, Annette. I'm back.'

Rain looked at the open door. Maybe he meant for her to follow him. She went inside. In a large room to the left, the three girls were sitting together on a settee.

Hayley was asleep with her thumb in her mouth. The other two were watching a video. Kerry put a finger to her lips as Tony was about to speak. 'Hayley's only just gone to sleep,' she whispered. Then she saw Rain. She jumped up from the settee and tiptoed over to her. Rain stared at the room. It was an incredible mess. Toys and books were scattered all over the carpet and the furniture. There were piles of clothes in one corner, on the floor and stacked precariously on an ironing board. There were towers of videos on top of the TV.

Kerry slipped her hand into Rain's and they followed Tony towards the back of the house. There were more piles of clothes stacked up in the hallway, and bags of shopping that hadn't been unpacked yet. In the kitchen, Daniel was washing up.

'I'm sorry, Dan. I . . .' Tony began.

'One o'clock, you said.' Daniel didn't look round. He rinsed off a plate and put it on the rack to drain. 'I should have finished my homework by now. You promised, Dad.'

He turned round, and saw Rain. His arms were covered with foam and he had a blue apron on. His face started turning red. *I should never have come here*, thought Rain.

Daniel looked exhausted. Just for a second, looking at Daniel and his dad side by side, Rain had the odd feeling that it was Daniel who was the grown-up.

'You should have come and got me,' Tony complained.

'So you fixed our car, then?' Daniel said. 'Mum can use it to go to work next week?'

'I'll start as soon as I've had some lunch. It won't take long . . .'

'Oh, great, Dad. So I have to look after the little ones all day? Thanks a bunch. So when do I do my homework? When do I . . . when do I do anything else?'

Daniel ran past Rain without looking at her, but that didn't stop her seeing the tears in his eyes. She wasn't sure what to do. She looked around the kitchen, and she couldn't believe what she saw. It was even more of a mess than the rest of the house. Every surface was stacked with things. Magazines, letters, newspapers, shopping, teapots, cups, dolls . . .

Tony tried half-heartedly to clear a space on the table, but he only made the mess worse. Rain couldn't stand watching him. 'I'll do it,' she said. She began to put some of the magazines in a pile.

'Don't worry about Daniel,' Tony said. 'He'll be all right in a bit.'

Who are you kidding, Rain thought.

'It's all been a bit of a nightmare. Annie's out at work a lot . . .' Rain remembered the angry woman outside the garage. '. . . and they're moving into the garage on Monday. Knocking it down. It's going to be a housing estate, would you believe? I've got to get all my stuff out, what's left of it.' Tony was opening and closing cupboards as he spoke. 'Where's the bread? There must be some here somewhere.'

'It's there,' Rain told him, pointing at the loaf balanced on top of the microwave. Tony grabbed the packet and it fell open. Slices of bread cascaded onto the floor. He swore.

'Dad!' said Kerry.

Tony paid no attention. He picked up the slices and jammed them into an overflowing rubbish bin, then he used what was left in the packet to make two cheese sandwiches. 'It's got a bit out of hand,' he said, when he saw Rain looking at the piles of clutter. 'It's a job to know where to start.'

Kerry tugged at Rain's arm. 'Will you come and play with my Barbies?' she said.

'Is that OK?' Rain asked Tony. She wondered where Daniel had gone.

'Whatever,' Tony said. Rain looked back as Kerry led her into the front room. Tony was sitting there in the middle of all the mess, staring into his teacup.

Hayley was just waking up, and she laughed when she saw Rain. Kerry started hunting under the cushions of the settee for Barbies and soon the girls had six of them sitting in a circle on the floor.

'Are you supposed to do that?' Rain asked Annette. She was snipping carefully at the hair of a Barbie in a long wedding dress.

'Mummy lets us,' said Kerry.

Rain didn't believe her, so she went to look for Tony. The kitchen was empty. There was a dining room at the back, not that anyone could ever have eaten in there. It was full of boxes of car parts and tools. There was no sign of Tony, though, so Rain went upstairs and picked her way through the jumble of roller skates and soft toys that covered the landing. She heard music coming from one of the rooms and she knocked on the door. It swung open and there was Daniel, sitting at a desk. When he saw Rain, he pushed what he was doing under a magazine. Only he wasn't quick enough.

'You were drawing,' she said.

Daniel went bright red. 'I was doing my homework.'

'We didn't *have* drawing for homework.'

'Who said you could come in here anyway? Who asked you to come round? Go on, get out.'

'I . . . I'm sorry. I only wanted to . . . I mean, I thought it would be OK to come and see you. I didn't expect . . .' As she spoke, Rain was taking in the details of Daniel's bedroom. Considering what the rest of the house was like, Daniel's room was amazing. It was tidy. There was a shelf of books over his bed, a computer on his desk, along with a neat stack of school files. Nothing on the floor, a couple of posters on the wall, no mess anywhere. The only thing out of place was a jamjar on his desk, with a few wild flowers in it.

'You didn't expect what?'

Rain didn't know what to say. Then she remembered why she'd come up here. 'I was playing with your sisters. But they're playing this game. With their dolls . . .'

'Barbie hairdressers? I shouldn't worry. They do worse things than that. And if they're doing that, they'll probably be happy for half an hour.'

'So what else do they do, then?'

He started telling her. The more he said, the more Rain realized how much time he must spend looking after them. 'It's like living with a demolition crew,' he said. 'But I never let them in here.'

'I can see that.' Daniel wasn't red any more. He was back to the pale, tired look. 'Are you going to show me what you were drawing, then?' Rain asked him.

'You'll laugh at it.'

'I look at drawings all the time. Max, my mum, she's a painter. And besides, no one could draw worse than me. I'm useless at it.'

Daniel lifted the magazine and showed Rain the sketch-pad lying underneath. He'd been drawing the flowers. She turned the page before he could reach out and stop her. The flowers were good, but now she was looking at something wonderful. It was Hayley, fast asleep with her thumb in her mouth. You could almost hear her breathing. 'Why do you want to hide these?' Rain asked him. 'They're fantastic.'

She looked up at him. He'd gone red again. He grabbed the pad from her hands.

'I knew I shouldn't have let you see. And you're wrong. They're not that good. There's things wrong with all of them.'

Rain laughed. 'You're nuts,' she said. 'If I could draw like that . . .' She stopped. 'You should show these to Max,' she told him.

'You're not listening. They're no good. She'd laugh at me.'

'No, she wouldn't. In fact . . .' Rain was about to tell him she'd seen one of his drawings already, the one of her, but what would he think if he knew she'd gone back and rescued it from the bin? It was her turn to blush.

'What?' said Daniel.

'You should do what *you* want sometimes, that's all,' she said, talking to cover her embarrassment. 'You shouldn't have to look after your sisters all the time. And you should stop playing football. Anyone can see you hate it.'

Rain knew she'd said too much before the words were out of her mouth. 'You don't understand anything,' Daniel said. He was angry. Really angry. 'Dad loves football. I do it for him, OK? I'm just no good at it, that's all. I'm no good at anything.'

He was right about one thing, Rain

thought. It was none of her business. Her face felt hot as she turned and went out of the door. Then she heard a yell from below. Daniel pushed past her and went down the stairs in two leaps. Rain followed him. Hayley was screaming and Daniel picked her up. 'What happened?' he demanded.

'We didn't do anything,' said Kerry.

'Kerry . . . cut . . . my hair,' gasped Hayley, between sobs.

'I never,' said Kerry. 'It was Annette. And anyway, Hayley wouldn't let us.' Kerry began to cry, and Annette joined in.

'Stop it!' yelled Daniel. 'All of you, just shut up!' But the girls cried even more. None of them heard the key in the front door.

'What on earth . . .?' Daniel's mum stood in the doorway. 'What's going on? Where's Dad?' Then she saw Rain and rearranged her face into a smile. 'Daniel? Who's this then? A friend?'

Daniel didn't say anything, so Rain said, 'I'm Rain. I go to Daniel's school.'

Hayley stretched out her hands to her mum. Mrs Moore put down a bag of shopping and took her from Daniel's arms. Kerry and Annette stopped crying, and Kerry said, 'Rain lives in a bus.'

'Not any longer,' Rain said.

'I'm hungry, Mum,' said Kerry.

'Me too,' said Annette.

'All right, all right,' said Mrs Moore. 'Give me a chance. Where *is* Dad?' she asked Daniel again.

'How should I know?' Daniel said. His mum looked at him sharply, but the girls were dragging her towards the kitchen.

'I'd better go,' said Rain. 'It's getting late. I . . . I'll see you Monday, yeah?'

Daniel turned away without replying and climbed slowly up the stairs. Rain heard his bedroom door close. She was alone in the cluttered hallway. She picked her way outside, and stood in the garden for a few moments feeling helpless in the face of so much unhappiness. Then she climbed on her bike and started to ride away, but something made her stop and look back. Just for a second she saw Daniel's face at his bedroom window, staring after her.

8

Rain arrived home to the smell of cooking. There was an unfamiliar table in the kitchen, and some new chairs. There was another smell too, which puzzled her until she realized it was the faint scent of Simon's aftershave. For a moment she wondered if he was still there, but he wasn't and she was glad about that. While Max cooked their supper, Rain told her about her visit to Daniel's house. She still felt shaken by the experience. But in the middle of it all there had been something good. She told Max about Daniel's drawings. 'Honestly, Max, you ought to see them.'

'I'd like to. It sounds like he's having a rough time. You should invite him round.'

'Yeah, well, I'm not sure if he'd come. I said some things I shouldn't have.'

'It can't have been that bad.'

'I don't know,' Rain said.

After they'd eaten they sat at the table as the candles flickered and moonlight flooded in through the open door. It was more like sitting in a cave than a house, with the smell of wood smoke drifting in from the remains of the fire outside. Then, just as Rain was starting to relax, just as she was starting to feel calm again, Max started talking about Simon's farm. 'He's even planning to work some of it with horses,' she said. 'Maybe all of it one day.'

'Great,' said Rain. Max talked on, telling her more about Simon's plans. Rain stopped listening. She couldn't make sense of the feelings that were tumbling around inside her. She should be interested in the farm. It sounded like Simon had loads of great ideas. But hearing Max going on about it this way . . .

'I'm tired,' she said, when Max paused for a moment. 'I think I'll go to bed.' She climbed the stairs to her new bedroom. She lay there for a long time, watching the moon shadows move across the walls, thinking, before she finally fell asleep.

When she woke up the following morning she couldn't work out where she was. 'Come on,' said Max, shaking her gently. 'I want to get going.'

'What . . . ?' Rain rubbed her eyes, staring at the white walls and ceiling.

'The light's perfect,' Max said. 'It's time I did some real work. I want to paint those marshes, the ones behind your school. But we need to go now. Grab yourself something to eat while I load the van.'

They drove up the lane, and Rain listened guiltily to the sound of the van's engine. She knew if she didn't look at it soon there'd be trouble. They turned onto the main road, and they'd gone about two miles when Rain saw the blue estate car on the verge with the bonnet up.

'Max!' she said. 'Pull over. That's Daniel.'

Max sighed, but she stopped the van, and Rain jumped out.

'What's the problem?' she asked Daniel.

'We were going to the match. Only we've broken down.' Daniel looked tense, nervous.

Tony stood up and slammed the bonnet down angrily. 'I don't believe it,' he muttered. 'We've run out of petrol.'

Rain stifled a laugh. 'We've got some in the van,' she told him.

Daniel watched her as she poured petrol into the tank. 'I'm sorry about yesterday,' she said, looking up. 'Are you OK?'

'Why wouldn't I be?'

'I just thought . . .'

'Leave it, all right? We're going to the match. Everything's fine.'

'Where is this match then?'

'By the school,' Daniel said. 'Where you saw us before.'

Rain had hardly screwed the petrol cap back on when Tony started the engine. 'Get a move on, Dan,' he said. 'We're late already.'

Daniel got in the car. He looked up at Rain through the open window. 'Look, I'm sorry,' he said quickly. 'I didn't mean . . .' But the end of his sentence was drowned by the roar of the car pulling away.

Max shook her head. 'People say *I'm* rude,' she said. 'You'd think he'd be grateful.'

When they arrived at the crossroads by the playing field Rain said, 'You can let me out here. I'd like to watch the match.'

'You're not serious?'

'You'll be ages, won't you? I'd just be sitting there.'

'That's never been a problem before.'

'It's not a problem. I'd just like to watch this match, OK? If I get bored I'll come and find you.'

'Fair enough,' said Max after a pause. 'You know where I'll be.'

Rain walked in through the gates. A bunch of spectators stood by the side of the pitch. The match had already begun, and Tony was standing with the coach – the little man in glasses who'd been yelling his head off the last time Rain had been here. He was yelling now.

Rain sat down on a swing and watched Daniel. He hardly touched the ball. None of them passed to him, and it looked as if he didn't care. At half-time, the coach led the boys to a spot close to where Rain was sitting. She tried to pretend she wasn't there, but she needn't have worried – they weren't interested in her. The coach shouted: 'You! Daniel! You have to get into that full-back.'

'Foul him. Is that what you mean?'

'Get stuck in, Daniel. You've hardly touched the ball.'

Daniel looked away. As soon as the game started again, the coach began to yell. 'GET BACK THERE, DANIEL! COME ON, CHASE HIM. GET STUCK IN!'

Rain walked over to the edge of the pitch and saw Daniel shrug his shoulders. Then, suddenly, the ball flew towards him. He controlled it, and began to run with it. One of the players from the other side ran after him, panting. Rain heard Tony shout, 'Go on, Daniel!'

Daniel looked up, and paused for a second too long. The defender slid in, tackled him, and raced away with the ball at his feet. Daniel was spread-eagled in the mud. Tony screamed at him. Rain flinched at the anger in his voice.

'GET UP, DANIEL! CHASE BACK. YOU LOST IT. YOU WIN IT BACK. GET AFTER HIM.'

Daniel was only a few metres from them. As he climbed to his feet Rain heard the coach's voice. 'God, he's useless!'

Daniel heard him, too. Rain saw his face change. She saw him turn and sprint back towards his own half. The other player had stopped near the halfway line, looking around.

'GO ON, THEN!' screamed the coach. 'TAKE HIM, LAD!'

Rain found herself yelling too. 'NO, DANIEL! NO!' But even if Daniel had heard her, it would have been too late. He couldn't have stopped himself if he'd wanted to. He leaped towards the ball with both feet and missed it completely. Rain heard, almost felt, his studs crunch into the shin of the other player. Then he thudded to the ground. When he sat up, Rain saw the other boy's leg. There was blood everywhere. For one sickening moment she thought that the leg was broken. The boy's face was white, and there were tears of pain in his eyes. People carried him carefully to the side of the pitch.

The spectators watching on the touchline were all shouting angrily. They were obviously the mums and dads of the other team. All except Tony. 'That kid's a menace,' spat a big man in a tracksuit.

'Too right,' agreed a woman in a baseball hat. 'He should be banned.'

'You don't know what you're talking about,' said Tony. 'He went for the ball.'

'Have you seen Gerry's leg?' demanded the woman. 'Have you *seen* it?'

The man in the tracksuit shoved her out of the way. 'Leave this to me, Tracey,' he said. He towered over Tony. 'Just you say that again. Go on, say it again.'

If the referee hadn't blown his whistle, Rain was sure there would have been a fight. But now they all watched Daniel getting shakily to his feet.

'Send him off, ref,' yelled the big man. There was a chorus of agreement from the rest of them. The ref walked over. 'If you don't keep your voices down,' he said, 'I shall report both your clubs to the league.' He walked back to Daniel.

'That was a dreadful tackle, lad,' he said. 'Terrible. I don't have any choice, you know.' He held up a red card, and a few people started to cheer, but the ref shot them a look and they stopped. Daniel walked away with his head down. As the match restarted, the coach came over to Tony.

'That settles it, then,' he said. 'I can't have a lad like that in the team, even if you did sponsor the shirts.' Rain had been wrong about his normal voice. He didn't shout, but he talked like a radio with the volume turned right up. All the faces turned to watch.

'It was an accident, Phil,' began Tony. 'And anyway, you've trained them to play that way.'

'Yeah, fine. Blame me. I don't care, Tony. We've got a new sponsor anyway. See you.'

For the second time that morning, Rain thought Tony was going to hit someone. His

106

face was white, absolutely white. He turned away suddenly and walked off towards the changing rooms. Rain didn't know what to do. She started walking after Tony, but he hadn't gone far when Daniel appeared. Daniel saw his dad, saw Rain, then dropped his bag on the ground and started to walk away.

'Daniel, wait,' Tony called after him. 'Where are you going? It wasn't your fault.'

Daniel turned round. He didn't stop, but kept walking backwards, away from them, as he spoke. His eyes were red. 'Don't be stupid. Of course it was my fault. I wanted to show Phil, I wanted to show all of you. And then I couldn't stop myself. I could have broken his leg.'

He turned and walked away quickly, half running, past the rusty car and out of the gate. Tony sat down on the bench outside the changing room and put his head in his hands. 'I'll go after him,' Rain said. 'I'll make sure he's OK.'

She ran out of the gate and saw Daniel turn down the lane that led to the marshes. She walked quickly but she didn't catch up with him, and she was just starting to think that maybe she should go back and wait at the playing field when she turned a corner and saw him.

Max had set up her easel overlooking the marshes. She was there now, and Daniel was standing beside her. They were talking, absorbed. They didn't even notice Rain arriving.

Daniel was staring at the huge sheet of paper that was pinned to Max's easel. The lines on the paper were delicate, but strong. Even though Rain had seen this kind of thing a million times before, it still took her breath away. It was so completely *Max*. The marsh and the fields and the sky were all there in those few lines. It was the way Max saw the world, and somehow she managed to get it down on paper, so that when you looked from the drawing to the real thing and back again, you saw things in a different way.

Only not everyone understood Max's pictures. People were always stopping to look over her shoulder when she was working. Nine times out of ten, they looked away again, disappointment in their faces. Max's pictures weren't like photographs. If people said anything it was usually, *What's that supposed to be, then?*

'Are you sure you're OK?' Max asked Daniel. She looked worried. Daniel's face was still pale and muddy. There were white streaks on it where tears had washed the mud away. He was a mess. But he was still gazing at the drawing. He shook his head. 'How do you do that?' he asked. 'It's fantastic.'

He looked up from the picture and Rain saw him snap back to reality. He stared blankly at her, and then seemed to sway on his feet. His face went a shade paler. Max stood up and pushed him gently into the chair. She unscrewed her battered flask and poured a cup of tea. 'Here,' she said. 'Drink this. Go on.'

Daniel sipped. His hands gradually stopped trembling.

'So, what happened?' asked Max.

'I tackled this kid,' Daniel said. 'In the match back there. His leg's really bad. It was my fault.' He shivered and swallowed a mouthful of tea. They could hear the faint sound of shouting back on the playing field.

'I'm sure it was an accident. These things happen in football matches, don't they?'

Daniel looked at Rain. 'Rain knows,' he said. 'I'd better go.'

109

'Just tell me though,' said Max. 'My drawing. What do you think?'

'Come off it. You don't need me to tell you.'

'I just wondered, that's all.'

'I think it's . . . I don't know what to say. I wish I could do that.'

'Rain told me you like drawing. She says you've been doing some at home. Look, why don't you show me what you've been doing? Bring it over. You know where we live.'

Daniel wasn't pale any more. The red started at his neck and rose slowly over his face. He gave Rain an angry look, as if to say, *How could you?* 'You wouldn't want to see them,' he said to Max. 'I couldn't.'

'I already—' Max began. Rain realized that Max was about to say she'd already seen one of his drawings. But she never finished. Tony pulled up beside them and pushed the passenger door open. Daniel took one look at his dad's face, and got into the car. Tony drove a little further down the lane, then reversed into an opening and screamed back past them. Rain saw two pale faces staring out through the windscreen, and then they were gone in a cloud of blue smoke.

When they arrived back at the cottage Rain headed towards the bus. She had her hand on the door handle before she remembered that she didn't live there any more. She felt a wave of sadness as she noticed the nettles that were already starting to grow up around the wheels. 'What's going to happen to it?' she asked Max.

'Simon says we can store it in one of his barns. If we keep it for fifty years it might be worth something. Or maybe we could put it into an exhibition of painted buses.'

'How can you laugh about it?' said Rain. 'Don't you feel sad?'

'Not really. We've done that thing. We're doing something else now. It's no good looking back. I've just got a few more things to move into the studio then Simon's coming to tow the bus away. D'you want to give me a hand?'

'I've got to do my homework,' Rain said. She went upstairs to her room. Max had helped her make shelves for her books from planks and bricks. The books were like old friends, but they looked uncomfortable and a little lost with so much white space around them.

Rain settled down to write up the details of the science experiment they'd done on Friday. It hadn't seemed much like an experiment to her. It wasn't as if they'd found anything out. Their experiment was supposed to be exactly the same as the one Mr Barry had done. And now she had to write out what she'd done all over again for homework.

'But I've already written it,' she'd said.

'Are you trying to cause trouble?' The teacher had just spent half an hour dealing with several kids who definitely *were* trying to cause trouble, so he wasn't in a good mood.

'No,' Rain had replied. 'I just wondered why I had to do it again.'

'Because I say so,' Mr Barry had snapped. 'Is that OK with you?'

Rain flipped back through the pages of the book. It hadn't all been bad. They had two different teachers for science, and the other one, Mrs Knox, was completely different from Mr Barry. With Mrs Knox they had designed their own experiments to test how well paper kitchen towels worked. Rain looked at her neat tables of results, and her careful diagrams. She smiled, remembering the mess that everyone had made – there had been water everywhere. Mr Barry didn't like mess. He liked neatness. *Right then*, thought Rain, *I'll show you*. She settled down to make a perfect job of the homework.

She had just finished when she heard the sound of Simon's tractor outside. She looked out of the window and saw Simon and Max fixing a heavy chain to the front of the bus, their heads close together as they worked. She ran downstairs and out into the garden.

'I need to check,' she said. 'In case I've left anything.'

Simon laughed. 'It's not going far, you know. And it *is* empty.'

Rain climbed inside. It was true. There was nothing left inside that was any use. She went and stood by the painted patch of wall where her room used to be. It was just an empty bus, scarred where Max had removed the cooker and the sink, and the wooden bed platforms. She went outside.

'You want one last ride?' Max asked.

Rain shook her head. Max got into the driver's seat and Rain watched as the chain tightened between the tractor and the bus, and the wheels began to move. Then they were gone. There was a rectangle of pale yellow grass that seemed too small. She still felt as if she'd left something inside the bus.

She went into Max's new studio. Now that all the junk was gone, the shed seemed far bigger. Max had painted the inside white, and cleaned the long windows that ran down the sides. The new shelves on one wall were crowded with jars and bottles full of pigments and liquids. The paint-spattered table from the bus stood at one side, Max's brushes laid out neatly on the surface, jars of pens and pencils ready. A truly enormous canvas was waiting, empty, on the easel at the far end. Max must have stretched it up that morning.

Max thinks our lives are like that, Rain thought. If you want to change something, just paint it out with brilliant white and start all over again. She'd seen Max do that when a painting had gone wrong. And she'd painted the house white, too, every centimetre. The bus was gone and every-thing was going to be new. It was what Max always said – don't look back.

Rain remembered what Max had said about her dad. *I never even think about him.* I don't want to be like that, Rain thought. It was *good*, living in the bus. I won't just forget about it. I won't forget the good bits *or* the bad bits. It's part of me. There's nothing wrong with looking back.

Bells Green was the first stop for the school bus. The second stop was in the village, out-side the garage. Rain was shocked when they pulled up and she saw that men had already started work there. There was a crane with a wrecking ball, two JCBs, and strips of fluorescent orange plastic all around the site. Rain couldn't imagine how Tony would be feeling.

Daniel got on the bus and walked straight past her to a seat near the back. Rain could see from his face that something was badly wrong so she got up and went to sit beside him. 'Are you going to move that bag, then?' she said.

Daniel didn't answer, and he left the bag where it was, so Rain sat in the seat in front of him. He was staring out of the window. 'It's a shame,' she said, as they pulled away from the demolition site. 'Your dad must be gutted.'

Daniel mumbled something. Rain thought she hadn't heard him properly. 'You what?'

'I said he's gone. OK? You satisfied now?'

'What do you mean? Gone where?'

'How should I know?' Rain waited, and suddenly words started spilling out of Daniel's mouth. 'When we got home yesterday after football and I told Mum what had happened, she just went crazy. I mean, they've had fights before, but never anything like that. They were shouting and swearing at each other, and the little ones started crying, so I took them to the playground, and when we got back, Dad was gone.'

He was blinking back tears. He turned away and wiped his face on his sleeve. The bus was coming into the next village now and Rain could see the crowd of kids jostling at the bus stop. 'I'm sorry,' she said quietly. The doors hissed open and kids began to rush up the aisle, ignoring the driver's threats.

When they arrived at school, a gang of

boys were waiting for Daniel. They surrounded him in the playground. 'We lost, thanks to you,' said Stephen. 'We had no chance when we were down to ten men.'

Daniel walked past them, but they followed him into the classroom, jostling him, not giving him any space. Everyone was talking about what had happened at the match. Rain heard Charlene saying, 'Yeah, he lost it, totally. He nearly killed the other boy. My friend says they were talking about calling the police. He's useless.'

Rain felt anger boiling inside her. They were pathetic, all of them. She thought of Daniel looking after his sisters, trying to keep everything together at home, and now it seemed as if his whole life was falling apart and all they could do was pick on him. The door opened. Mrs Haynes walked in and the talking stopped. Rain looked over to see how Daniel was handling it. He was staring ahead, white-faced.

The first lesson that day was double maths, and there was a supply teacher. He picked up the black folder on his desk, looked inside it, and then said, 'You can either sit and do six pages from your textbook, or we can do something interesting. Your choice.'

All around the room people sat up and looked at him. 'Right then,' he said. 'Something interesting it is. Anyone know what fractals are?'

'I do,' said Rain.

She hadn't put her hand up, but this teacher didn't seem bothered by that. 'What do you know about them?' he asked.

'I'm interested in Chaos theory,' Rain said, ignoring the laughter from the rest of the class. 'There's some things I think I understand, but I don't see how equations can make pictures.' As she spoke she was thinking of the pictures painted on the side of the bus. A crazy long-haired hippie called Rabbit had painted them. 'Fractals, man!' he'd told Rain with a gleam in his eyes. 'The pattern of the universe.' And when she'd bought the book about Chaos she'd seen them again. 'There's something called the Mandelbrot set, I think,' she said.

'Boring,' said a voice. It was Stephen as usual.

'Yeah, right,' said someone else. 'I thought you said this was going to be interesting.'

For a moment Rain thought that this

lesson was going to go the way of a lot of the others. A war of words between an angry teacher and kids who didn't care. But this teacher was different. He opened his briefcase and took out a wad of long narrow strips of paper. He handed them round. 'Fold them in half,' he said. 'Now do it again . . . and then twice more.'

'There's nothing left,' someone joked.

'What's the point?' asked someone else.

'Unfold it and stand it on its side,' the teacher said. 'Now crease each fold into a proper right angle.'

Rain worked carefully. The strip of paper turned into a strange, elegant shape of squares and half-squares on the table. It was nothing like she had expected. 'So what would happen if you folded it one more time?' asked the teacher. He had everyone's attention now. 'Go on,' he said. 'Get another piece of paper and try it.'

The paper was hard to fold so small, but amazingly, everyone was trying to do it – even Stephen. When Rain had finished, she had a shape that was like the first one, but not like it. 'In a way,' the teacher said, looking at Rain, 'that's the answer to your question. You did something very simple to the paper. Then you did the same thing to what you'd already done. And you made a kind of picture.'

Rain felt a surge of excitement. This was the kind of thing she'd hoped would happen at school. It was like a new world opening up. 'What would the next one be like?' she wondered out loud. 'You couldn't fold the paper that small.'

'No.' The teacher was smiling. 'But maybe you could work it out. I see you're due for some homework, so have a go.'

There was a chorus of groans, and then the bell went.

'What are you trying to prove?' said Stephen. He was waiting for Rain outside the door. 'That you're cleverer than the rest of us? If you were clever, you'd keep your big mouth shut.'

'Yeah?' Rain was getting tired of all this. 'So what's the point of coming to school if you don't want to learn anything, then?'

'Exactly,' he said. 'Coming to school when you don't even have to, now that really is sad.' They all laughed.

Rain pushed past them. It seemed as if, every time something good happened, something else happened to spoil it. She went out into the playground where grey clouds were banked up in the sky, and a cold wind was blowing, keeping most people inside. It felt like winter, and a fine drizzle was starting to fall, but she didn't care. She sat on an empty bench and filled her lungs with clean air. The smell of school was something she didn't think she'd ever get used to – sweat, deodorant, dust, the used breath of a thousand people.

What would Max be doing? she wondered. Painting? Cooking? Or maybe, she thought, as her heart beat faster, maybe Max would be helping Simon. She could picture it, their heads together as they fixed the chain to the bus. Them laughing together. And she was here. Why am I doing this? she thought.

Then she saw Daniel. He was out on the field, walking away into the distance. She went after him and caught up with him by the fence on the far side. He didn't look at her, just stared through the wire. But he started talking.

'Mum says it's the best thing, Dad going. She said none of us could go on like that. But I keep thinking, if I hadn't done that stupid tackle, if I hadn't hurt that boy, at least Dad would still have had the football to look forward to, wouldn't he? So he wouldn't have gone.' He kicked the fence viciously. Then he said in a low voice, 'It's my fault he went. Nothing I do is any good. Nothing.'

There was a long silence. Daniel was gripping the wire of the fence so tightly that his knuckles were white. 'It's all my fault,' he repeated.

'You can't think that!' Rain burst out. 'You couldn't have done any more. All those times you've looked after your sisters. I bet if it wasn't for you, your house would be even more of a mess than it actually is. You probably wouldn't even be able to get through the door.'

Daniel picked up his bag. Rain wasn't sure he was even listening. 'And anyway,' she went on, 'you don't know he's gone for good.' Daniel looked at her then. 'Well?' she repeated. 'You don't, do you?'

'I don't know anything,' he said. 'Not any more.' He looked at his watch. 'But if we're late for PE, we'll get done."

He started walking towards the school. 'It's not true you're no good at anything,' Rain called after him. 'What about your drawing? You care about that. I saw your face when you were looking at Max's work.'

Daniel stopped walking then, and turned back. The rain had plastered his hair to his head and it was dripping from his eyebrows. 'Did your mum mean it?' he asked. 'Would she really help me?'

'She wouldn't have offered if she didn't mean it,' Rain said. 'Believe me, you're privileged. And I bet Mr Hogan would help you, too. He was dead impressed by that drawing.'

'You don't get it, do you?' Daniel said. 'About keeping them off your back?' Rain didn't have to ask who he meant by *them*. 'If you act all keen, then if they like you, maybe they'll just laugh. But if they hate you, like they hate me, or if you're . . . well . . . different, like you . . . they'll make your life hell.'

'You can't *be* like that,' Rain said angrily. 'You can't just give up. I mean, who cares what other people think? You should do what *you* want to do. What's wrong with being good at things? I *want* to be good at things. There's no point being here otherwise.'

'Because they won't leave you alone,'

Daniel said. 'Can't you see I'm trying to help you? All you have to do is try and fit in. I mean, you ask questions all the time in lessons. No one does that.'

'That's pathetic,' Rain said. She'd forgotten she was talking to someone whose dad had just walked out. 'And you don't keep them off your back anyway, do you? Before you said all this I was starting to wonder if it was worth all the hassle. I was feeling sorry for myself. Well, not any more. You know what? There's been times when we've been parked up in a lay-by somewhere and people have come in the middle of the night, thumping on the bus, yelling, revving their motorbikes. We've even had bricks through the window. Why would I care what a few spotty kids think of me? And actually,' she went on, 'believe it or not I've been doing my best to fit in. But that's obviously a waste of time. They're not going to like me whatever I do, are they?'

She walked off across the wet tarmac. The rain was coming down even harder now. She was halfway back to the school before she remembered she was meant to be feeling sorry for Daniel. He was still standing there, his hair dripping onto his sweatshirt.

'I'm sorry,' she said. 'It makes me mad, that's all. We'd better go in before we drown.'

Rain spotted the faces looking at them through the little squares of glass in the door long before they reached it. Stephen, Stacey and Marianne were waiting. 'He *is* your boyfriend, isn't he?' said Stacey.

Rain ignored her and carried on walking.

'Stuck-up bitch.' The words followed Rain down the corridor. *Ignore them*, she told herself. *Go on. You can do it*.

'That right?' she heard Stephen say to Daniel, sneering. 'She your girlfriend?'

Rain turned, in spite of herself. 'What would your *dad* say about your boyfriend, Rain?' demanded Stacey.

'Yeah,' said Marianne, 'I bet he'd think you're too young to have a boyfriend.'

'Oh, sorry, Rain,' Stacey laughed. 'You haven't got a dad, have you? I forgot.'

Rain didn't know what to say. She felt the anger rising in her. She looked at their laughing faces and wondered what it was that made them be like this – what it was about *her*.

'Right,' said Stephen. 'And maybe Daniel hasn't either, not any more. My sister's best friend lives next door to them. She says last night . . .'

Rain saw the look on Daniel's face. She couldn't understand how Stephen could be so cruel. She pushed Stacey out of the way and shoved Stephen against the wall. She saw surprise in his eyes, then panic. It served him right. She slapped him, hard, across the face.

'You. Come here!'

Rain saw a smile appear on Stephen's face. Mr Crawley, the deputy head, was walking towards them.

'I said, *come here*.'

'He was having a go at Daniel. They all were. They—'

Mr Crawley didn't let her finish. 'There are no possible excuses for violent behaviour,' he said. 'You know where my office is? Wait for me there.'

'But—'

'Just do it.'

It was a long way to Mr Crawley's office. It crossed Rain's mind that she could walk out of school and never come back. Then she thought about what she'd said to Daniel.

She'd told him it was pathetic to give up, so she kept on walking. Her hand was still stinging where she'd slapped Stephen. She knew there was going to be trouble, but once they understood what had happened she was sure they'd let her off with a detention – something like that.

She didn't have to wait long for Mr Crawley. He opened the door of his office and she went inside. 'We'll need to get your parents in at once,' he said. 'Phone number?'

'We haven't got one.'

'Don't be ridiculous. Don't think you can lie your way out of trouble.'

'It's true.'

He picked up the phone on his desk. 'Mr Crawley here. Could you find me a contact number for Rain Smith. She's in Year . . . Oh . . . right . . . I see.'

'Very well, then,' he said. 'I shall have to *write* to your parents. Once we've met we can decide on what further action is appropriate. In the meantime, you can write a letter of apology to Stephen. I must say that I have never seen such disgraceful behaviour from a girl at this school. Stephen has a nasty mark on his face, and

I'm not looking forward to explaining that to his parents. We simply can't tolerate this kind of behaviour.'

'Oh, right,' Rain said. Her anger had been growing during Mr Crawley's speech and now she could contain it no longer. 'You don't even want to hear my side of it? You don't want to know why I did it?' She was standing up now, and shouting.

'Sit down,' hissed Mr Crawley. 'I don't think you realize how serious this is. You struck another pupil. Are you saying he hit you first? No, I thought not. Well, I'll tell you now, young lady, unless you are extremely careful your short career at this school will be over.'

Rain didn't understand what he was saying to her. 'What do you mean?' she said. She felt hot, feverish, and her ears were buzzing.

'I mean that if we think it's necessary we will exclude you. Is that clear enough for you? So you'd better start writing, hadn't you?'

Rain wrote what Mr Crawley told her to write. She could see that he thought he'd beaten her. He didn't care about the truth, or being fair. He just wanted to win, to make her do what he wanted. Or maybe there was more than that. Maybe he was like some of the kids. Maybe he just didn't like her being there, the way Grandma didn't like the bus being parked outside her house. Well, whatever it was, she wasn't going to let him win.

When Rain had finished writing, Mr Crawley told her to go. 'Mrs Haynes will give you a letter to take home,' he said. 'Make sure you deliver it.'

Rain turned to open the door.

'Wait,' Mr Crawley said. 'What's that in your ear?'

Rain stopped. Her hand went up automatically to the tiny earring.

'The rule is, "No jewellery",' he said. 'Which part of that sentence don't you understand, exactly?'

Rain stared at him. She could just imagine what Max would say about him. *Little Hitlers*, she liked to call the pompous officials who'd sometimes come with papers, forcing them to move the bus. The tweed jacket Mr Crawley was wearing was a kind of uniform. 'Well?' he was saying. 'I'm waiting.'

All kinds of thoughts were rushing

through Rain's head. He couldn't possibly know how important that tiny sapphire was. It had been there in her ear since she was five years old. She'd never taken it out. Max had told her they'd make her take it out, and she'd been right. So, wasn't it giving in to take it out now? Wasn't it the first step to becoming the same as all the rest of them, just like Max had predicted? She looked at her black school uniform. She was wearing this. She'd taken all the other earrings out. It hadn't changed who she was inside, had it?

Her hands shook as she reached up and pulled the clip off the back of the earring. For a second, she thought it wasn't going to come out; then she was holding it, tiny, between her trembling fingers.

'Don't let me see that again,' Mr Crawley said, as she went out of the door.

When Rain came out of school, she heard the hooting straight away. Max was waiting in the van. For one bad moment she thought that the school must have found some way of getting in touch with her. She was about to cross the road when Mrs Haynes came up to her, holding a brown envelope. Her face was worried. 'You should have come to see me about this,' she said. 'I knew something was going on.'

'I can handle it,' Rain told her.

'Well, slapping Stephen Phillips isn't going to help you,' said Mrs Haynes, 'and neither is getting on the wrong side of Mr Crawley.' Rain looked at her. It didn't sound as if she liked Mr Crawley much. She handed Rain the envelope. 'You can talk to me, you know,' she said. 'Any time.'

Rain watched her go, and then crossed the road to the van.

'I had to get some brushes and some paints from town,' said Max. 'So I thought I'd pick you up. What was all that about? That woman looked dead serious.'

'Here.' Rain handed her the letter. Max ripped the envelope open and read. 'Is this right?' she said after a few seconds. 'You actually hit this kid? Why?'

'There was a gang of them. They started the day I arrived. They're pathetic, really. But today they were going on at Daniel, and his dad's left home, and I was so angry. Stephen deserved it.'

'It doesn't mention any of that here.'

'He didn't ask.'

'Right.' Max opened the door and started to get out.

'Max, wait. What are you going to do?'

'I'm going to sort this guy out. What do you think?'

'Max, don't. Please. Just wait.'

She closed the door again, then she said, 'I thought you told me school was absolutely fine?'

Rain didn't say anything for a moment. Then she said, 'OK, I admit it, you were right about some things. But now I've seen what it's like and I still want to do it. I can make it work.'

'Sure,' said Max. 'You wait till you've had a few years of it . . . a few months even.'

'I mean it, Max. And I'm not going to be a clone or a zombie or a sheep or any of those things. I'm going to be me. That's what I've decided, right.'

'That'll be why you've taken your earring out, then?'

Rain's stomach lurched. She'd meant to put it back when she was on the bus. She hadn't expected Max to pick her up. She fumbled in her pocket and started to put it back in.

'I knew it,' Max said as she started the

van. 'I knew they'd make you take it out. They won't stop until they control every little bit of you.'

When they got home Max went straight out to the studio. She'd bought some big new fluorescent lights that made it like daylight in there, so that she could work at night-time. And once she'd fixed up the lights she started work on her new painting. Rain cooked some pasta and made a tomato sauce with loads of garlic, and Max came in and ate when Rain called her. She didn't say anything, and Rain knew she was still upset about the earring. She didn't know how she could make Max see that taking an earring out didn't mean she was giving in, didn't turn her into a different person.

Max went back to work and Rain went up to her room. It felt strange, Max working in a different place. She was used to her presence in the bus. The house was empty around her.

She thought about what had happened at school, and wondered what it would be like the next day. She thought about Daniel, and his sisters, with their dad gone. She looked at the strip of photos she'd pinned up beside her bed, and wondered how she'd feel if her own dad had just left her. She took a book from the shelves and started to read, but she was so tired that the words blurred in front of her eyes. Before she knew it, she was asleep.

She was at school, walking out of the gate and she could hear their voices. 'Where's your dad, Rain? You haven't got a dad, have you, Rain?'

'He's over there. He's meeting me after school. Look, there's his car.' Rain could see the car, cruising to a stop outside the gate, but she couldn't see his face, and she heard Stacey saying, 'Don't be stupid, Rain, that's *my* dad.' Stacey pushed past her and went to open the door, but before she could open it the car glided away. Rain knew it was her dad in there, but Stacey had made him go away.

Pebbles crunched under her feet and a cold wind cut through her clothes. The buildings had gone and she was standing on a beach. It was winter, and waves were crashing on the rocks. He was there, standing on a rocky promontory. She ran towards him, but the pebbles slid beneath her feet, so that she felt as if she was running backwards. She *was* running backwards. She called out to him, but he couldn't hear her over the crash and roar of the breakers. Then he was gone.

Rain woke up, shaken by the intensity of the dream. The lights were still on in Max's studio and when she looked at her clock she saw that it was two in the morning. She put her pyjamas on and fell into a deep sleep. When she woke again it was eight o'clock and the sun was streaming in through the window. She ran downstairs.

'Why didn't you wake me?' she said to Max. 'I'll never catch the bus now.'

'There's no rush,' Max told her. She was reading the letter from school again. 'I'm taking you in,' she went on. 'I want to meet this bloke, Crawley.'

'The letter said four fifteen.'

'Yeah. But I'm not letting them push *me* around. I've got a feeling he'll see me. The guy obviously needs sorting.'

'Max, you won't make things worse, will you?'

'What do you mean?'

'I mean, I can sort out my own problems.'

'Sure. But *he* asked to see *me*, right?'

'I just think it'd be best if you just tell him you'll make sure I don't do it again. Say you want to help them.'

'And you're going to put up with him treating you like that? He'll never change if you do.'

'But if you cause trouble they might throw me out.'

'They won't do that.'

'Please, Max.'

Rain looked at her mum, but she didn't dare say any more. There were dark bags under Max's eyes. She'd obviously stayed up all night working. 'What have you been doing?' Rain asked her.

'The painting of the marshes. But you won't be interested in that.'

'Max!'

Rain went outside and walked across to the studio. It looked as if there had been a hurricane. Drawings were scattered everywhere, pinned to the walls, lying on the floor. At the end of the room the canvas had changed colour. The whole thing was now a rich, earthy red. Lines of charcoal snaked across it.

'Well,' asked Max. 'What do you think, then?'

'I thought you weren't interested in what I thought.'

'Well, now I'm asking you. Tell me.'

But Rain couldn't. With the drawings, she'd learned how to make sense of them, but the paintings were different. At the beginning they looked nothing like they would do later, as Max added layer after layer. It was all inside Max's head.

'I can't see it,' Rain said. 'Not when it's like this. But I like to see them grow. You know I do. And I'll know when it's finished.'

Max didn't reply. It was plain that she was in a terrible mood, and Rain was starting to dread what was going to happen when Max arrived at school. Max walked up to the canvas and rubbed at one of the lines with her finger. Then she picked up a stick of charcoal and started to draw.

'Max,' said Rain. She knew if she let her get started she wouldn't stop. 'You're taking me to school, remember?'

'Yeah, right.' She put the charcoal down and picked up a sheet of paper. It was Daniel's drawing. When she saw it, Rain remembered his face the day before, rain dripping from his hair. 'I told him you meant it about helping him,' she said. 'You did, didn't you?'

Max's face lit up for a moment. It was like the sun coming out on a stormy day. 'Oh, yes. I'm glad,' she said. 'Tell him to come over soon. I liked him. But what were you telling me about his dad? What happened?' Max pinned Daniel's drawing to the wall.

'There was some kind of row and his dad walked out. He was really upset. Then this boy Stephen started going on about it, needling him. It was vicious, Max.'

'And he's the one you hit?'

Rain nodded.

'Right, then,' Max said grimly. 'Let's go and see these people.'

The school entrance was crowded with buses and milling children. 'That's Mr Crawley, over there,' Rain said. 'He's on bus duty.'

'Great,' said Max, as she reversed the van quickly into a parking space. 'That'll save time. I'll see you later.'

'Max, wait.' Rain got out of the van and watched Max stride towards Mr Crawley

140

with the letter fluttering in her hand. She saw Mr Crawley glance at Max and then dismiss her as not worth his attention, which was a bad mistake. Max placed herself between him, and the group of boys he was telling off. He turned away again, trying to ignore her. The boys watched, open-mouthed. Rain hardly dared to think what Max might be saying to him. Mrs Snowley appeared from the main entrance of the school.

'Is that your mum?' The voice made Rain jump. Beth and Alice were standing behind her.

'What if it is?'

'Cool. Look at the Creep. He doesn't know what to do.'

Mrs Snowley was ushering Max and Mr Crawley into the school. Rain had a bad feeling, but there was nothing she could do about it now.

'Is it true, you hit Stephen?' asked Alice.

Rain nodded.

'It was about time someone stood up to him,' Beth said.

'Right,' agreed Alice.

'So why didn't they, then?' demanded Rain. 'Why didn't *you*?'

Alice looked at her, but Beth pulled at her arm. 'Come on,' she said. 'What's the point?'

Rain almost called after them that she didn't mean it, but she couldn't. She *did* mean it. And now they were walking away, and someone was calling her name. She turned and saw Mrs Snowley.

'You should all be in class by now,' she said. 'Alice, will you tell Mrs Haynes that Rain is with me, please? Come along, Rain.'

Mrs Snowley didn't speak on the way to her office. When she opened the door Rain saw Mr Crawley and Max, both sitting like statues on the edges of their chairs. Max looked like a bomb about to go off.

'Sit down, please, Rain,' Mrs Snowley said. She pointed to a chair between Max and Mr Crawley. Then she turned to Max. 'Ms Smith, we've asked you to come into school because Rain has been involved in a serious incident with another pupil . . .'

'She hit him, you mean.'

'Well, yes.'

'Then why don't you say so? And this guy here didn't even wonder why that happened?' She stabbed a finger towards Mr Crawley. Rain looked at her, willing her to calm down, but it was no good.

'Ms Smith . . .'

'Why do you keep calling me that? My name's Max.'

'Ms Smith,' repeated Mrs Snowley. She sounded as if she was talking to a child, Rain thought, and she knew the effect that would have on Max. 'Rain has hit another child. She has admitted it, and apologized, which is all very well as far as it goes. But in cases of violence or bullying, our governors have laid down very strict guidelines. This is the first time Rain has been in this kind of trouble, and I am reluctant to exclude her from school. As long as I know we have your full support in tackling her behaviour, I am prepared to take the less serious course of putting her on report. She'll have a book which her teachers will sign at the end of each lesson and—'

'This is a load of garbage.' Max was on her feet. Mrs Snowley went red. Rain could see what was going to happen, and she knew there was no way she could stop it. She glanced at Mr Crawley. He was sitting back in his chair looking pleased with himself. Max was in full flow now. 'You can't treat people like this. You think Rain would just hit someone for no reason? Nothing's changed, has it? Schools are just the same as they always were.'

'Please, Ms Smith, sit down.' Max walked across to the window. 'I do want to hear what Rain has to say,' Mrs Snowley continued. 'If you will just calm down and give us a chance. Now then, Rain?'

There was a silence. They all looked at Rain. 'It was Daniel,' she began. 'They were having a go at him because he—'

'Really,' sniffed Mr Crawley. 'I've been into all this, Mrs Snowley, with the children concerned. It was a storm in a teacup, or it was until this young lady took matters into her own hands.'

Rain caught a look on Mrs Snowley's face, just for a second, and knew that Mrs Snowley didn't trust what Mr Crawley was saying. For one tiny moment, she thought it was going to be OK. But then Max was striding past her. She towered over Mr Crawley. 'Are you calling my daughter a liar?' she hissed.

'Max,' Rain pleaded. 'Don't.'

'You're a smug, self-righteous toe-rag. You're not fit to be looking after kids. Come on, Rain. We're going.'

'But Max, I don't want—'

'You leave me no alternative,' Mrs Snowley was saying. 'I shall be excluding Rain for the rest of this week. After that it will be half-term, and—'

'You do what you like,' said Max. She had Rain by the hand and she was almost dragging her out of the door. 'I shouldn't think you'll have to endure Rain's presence any longer.'

And then they were out on the car park and Rain was sobbing. Her breath was coming in huge gasps and she was hitting Max and Max was holding her wrists trying to stop her.

'I hate you!' she screamed. 'I hate you. You've ruined everything.'

Max stormed off towards the van and Rain was left standing in the middle of the car park. She couldn't face going back into school, and there was no point anyway. There was no point in anything any more. She felt as if she had nowhere left to go.

And then she thought of Grandma.

Rain walked to the van and got in. Max was staring out through the windscreen, stony faced. When they arrived back at the cottage Rain went upstairs and threw a few clothes and her toothbrush into an old bag. She took a last look around her room. It didn't even *feel* like her room. There were the books and the bedspread, but her real bedroom was sitting forlornly in one of Simon's barns, its axles propped up on concrete blocks, going nowhere.

As she was leaving she noticed the strip of photographs of her dad. They were lying on her pillow where she'd been looking at them the night before. She picked them up and stuffed them in the top of her bag.

Downstairs, Max was standing in the kitchen and Simon was sitting on a chair. There was a smell of yeast. Max had started making the bread as if nothing had happened. It was one of Rain's jobs, making the bread, or it had been when they lived on the bus.

'Hi, Rain,' said Simon.

'What's *he* doing here?' she demanded. She didn't wait for an answer. Simon stood up awkwardly to let her past.

Max ran outside after her. 'Rain?' she said. 'Where are you going?'

Rain didn't reply. She walked out of the drive and across the green. There were ducks and moorhens everywhere, pecking at the wet grass. She felt Max's hand on her shoulder and shook it off, but Max grabbed her again, roughly, and spun her round.

'What do you think you're doing?'

'I'm getting away from *you*.'

'I was standing up for you. That's what I'm meant to do, isn't it? I'm your mother.'

'You weren't doing it for me. You weren't even thinking about me. It was just you and them. As soon as you go through that gate you start acting like they're all out to get you. I can't stand it any more. I'm going to Grandma's.'

Rain was shaking, but she turned round and started walking. She was sure Max would come after her. The lane was yellow with fallen leaves, and slippery. Some trees were completely bare now, and she could see the brown fields beyond them. The rain had stopped and cloud shadows were racing across the wet ploughland. Rain told herself not to look back, but at the corner where the trees ended, she couldn't stop herself. Max was still standing there, watching her.

She was nearly at the main road when she heard the van. It pulled up beside her and the door opened. 'Get in,' ordered Max.

'I can catch the bus.'

'You'll have a long wait. The next bus is on Friday morning.'

Rain kept walking, but Max edged the van forward.

'I'll take you to Grandma's,' she shouted over the clatter of the engine. Rain stopped, and Max switched the engine off. Crows were flapping like torn black paper above the fields, cawing. 'You're right,' Max said. 'It's the best thing. We both need a break. Come on. Get in.'

*　*　*

An hour later they were outside Grandma's house. Rain saw the curtain move in the window, and realized that Grandma wouldn't know who the rusty white van belonged to. She jumped out and ran to the front door.

'Rain?' said Grandma. 'What are you doing here? Who's that in the van? Where's Maxine?'

'It's our van, Grandma. The bus broke down and we've got a house now and I'm going to school, only—'

'Just hold on a moment,' said Grandma. 'Come inside and I'll get the kettle on, then you can tell me all about it properly. What on earth is Maxine doing?'

Max was still sitting in the van. Now she opened her door and walked up the path towards them. 'So you've finally seen reason,' Grandma said to her. 'You might have had the grace to let me know. You just tip up on my doorstep out of the blue, and—'

'It's great to see you too, Mum,' said Max. 'Rain wants to stay with you for a while.'

'Well, that's typical,' said Grandma. 'No warning, and you want to dump Rain on me as if she was a sack of potatoes. It's lucky for you I'm here. I should be meeting my friend for coffee. I'll have to call her.'

Rain and Max sat in Grandma's cluttered front room and drank tea. No matter how hard Rain tried, she couldn't imagine Max growing up here. There were photographs of Max on the mantelpiece, but they were all pictures of a little girl. In one, Max was on a beach in a swimsuit, digging in the sand with a tall man in glasses helping her. That was Grandad. He had died when Rain was five. There was a family portrait where Max was wearing a flowery dress, sitting between her mum and dad. Rain had never seen Max in a dress. Right now, she was sitting on the edge of her chair in her paint-spattered overalls while Grandma tried to interrogate her. Max put her cup down and stood up. 'Rain can tell you about it,' she said. 'I've got to go.'

'But you've only just arrived. And what about Rain? How long is she staying?'

'You'd better ask her,' said Max. 'This was her idea.'

Rain could see that Max was agitated and upset. She could see that she wanted to get out before she had a fight with Grandma. She was out of the door now, standing on the pavement, and Rain wanted to run to her and tell her it was all a mistake and throw her arms around her because she could see she was feeling hurt, but Max didn't give her the chance. She jumped into the van and drove away. Rain listened to the sound of the clapped-out engine fading into the distance and then followed Grandma indoors.

'We'll have to make some plans,' Grandma said brightly. 'There are plenty of things we can do. A trip to the seaside. A little shopping. I really wasn't expecting this. I'll have to rearrange a few things . . .' She paused as something occurred to her. 'But shouldn't you be at school? It's not half-term yet, is it? Rain? What's the matter?'

Rain didn't mean to cry, but a feeling of loneliness washed over her. Things kept happening and none of them made any sense. She wanted Max and Max wasn't here and she'd made it all happen somehow. Grandma sat her down and made her drink hot sweet tea, and Rain tried to explain what had been going on.

'Well,' said Grandma when she had finished. 'We'd better see about getting you back to this school of yours, hadn't we?'

'They won't let me go back. You didn't hear what Max said to them.'

'No, but I can imagine. I'm not Maxine though, am I? At least let me telephone this Mrs Snowley.'

When Grandma came back into the room, Rain didn't need to ask what Mrs Snowley had said. One look at Grandma's face was enough. 'I'm going to go and see them,' Grandma said. 'I'll *make* them see reason.'

'Grandma, it doesn't matter. It's only a few days and then it's half-term. No one's said I can't go back ever, have they?' *Except*, she thought, *that was exactly what Max wanted. Wasn't it?* She felt so tired.

'I'm sorry, Rain,' said Grandma, sitting down beside her. 'You've had a tough day. Let's go and sort your room out. Come on. Is this all you've brought?' She picked up Rain's battered rucksack. 'I can see we'll have to go shopping.'

Rain followed her upstairs and pushed open the door of the spare room. 'You run yourself a bath,' Grandma said, 'and I'll put your things away for you.'

'It's OK,' Rain began, but Grandma already had the bag open. The strip of photographs fell out onto the bed. Grandma picked it up.

'What's this?' she asked.

'It's a picture of my dad. Max gave it to me.'

'I thought . . . I didn't know Maxine had told you about him. She always said—'

'That we didn't need him?' Grandma nodded. 'Well, I wanted to know. So I asked her. And she found this for me.'

'He was a nice boy,' said Grandma. 'He had a good head on his shoulders. This isn't typical.' She lifted the pictures and squinted at them. 'I thought Maxine would calm down once she'd met him.'

'She didn't though, did she?'

Grandma shook her head. 'Maxine wouldn't let him see you, you know. In the hospital. Your grandad and me, we tried to persuade her. Your grandad got angry. Next thing we knew she was away in that bus.' Grandma was still holding the photos. 'I've got a much better picture than this,' she said hesitantly. 'Would you like to see it?'

Rain looked sharply at her. There was something else, something she wasn't saying. Grandma went out of the room for a moment, and returned almost immediately with a picture in a gold frame. A sun-tanned face with something familiar about it, smiling. Short hair. Open-necked shirt. Rain put it beside her dog-eared strip of pictures. She would never have known it was the same person. This man was older, neater, more ordinary.

'Where did you get this?' she asked.

'I'll make us something to eat,' said Grandma. 'We can talk later.'

But they didn't talk later. Grandma chattered about a hundred different things, they watched TV, and then Grandma bustled Rain off to bed.

Rain dreamed again. She was on a sofa, watching TV. Kerry and Annette were beside her, and Hayley was asleep on her lap. She could smell the tea cooking. Max was in the kitchen, and Dad would be home soon. She heard the key in the front door, so she lifted Hayley gently and stood up as Simon appeared in the doorway. But then it wasn't Simon, it was Tony. He was wearing his oil-stained red overalls and his arms were full of cogs. They were spilling onto the floor. Rain heard herself saying, 'Dad?'

'I'm having trouble with the gearbox,'

Tony said. The cogs were spilling everywhere. Rain scrabbled on the floor, trying to pick them up. Some of them were tiny, so tiny that she could hardly see them. She knew there were others that were completely invisible. She heard Daniel's voice and she turned to see him kneeling beside her. 'It's useless,' he said. 'We'll never find them all.' And Rain said, *We have to. We have to.* But Max was calling her. Max was going somewhere. She was leaving . . .

Rain woke up, damp with sweat. Grandma's central heating. She got out of bed and opened the window. Outside, the wind was rushing through the treetops, blasting more leaves from the branches. She gulped the air into her lungs and stared out into the night. The wildness and the wetness and the darkness felt like home to her in a way that she knew the four walls of a house never would. Living in a bus, you could never forget the weather. You heard every drop of rain that fell, shuddered through every gale. And when they weren't in the bus, which was most of the time, they were out in the open air. Most of Rain's life had been spent outdoors.

She got back into bed and fell asleep with the sound of the wind in her ears and Max's voice in her head singing nursery rhymes, the way she always used to do when Rain was little and the wind was shaking the bus, and she was scared.

13

Rain stayed with Grandma for more than a week, and it was one of the busiest weeks of her life. Every morning Grandma made a picnic, and they drove off on a frantic tour of museums and wildlife centres, castles and shopping malls. All day, every day, Grandma talked, chattered, about absolutely nothing. TV programmes, the state of the roads, the weather, the price of ham. But Rain knew it was all a front. There was something she wasn't saying.

Grandma waited until the last night. They'd spent the afternoon on a boat looking at seals, and it was easily the best thing they had done. There had been wild salt marshes and miles and miles of sand and sea and sky.

'Back home tomorrow,' Grandma said, over prawn salad for tea. Earlier in the week she'd made Rain send Max a postcard. It was the first time she'd ever written to her, except for birthday cards. She hadn't known what to say, and in the end she'd scribbled: *Back Saturday. See you then. Love Rain.*

'It's been fun, hasn't it?' Grandma said. She was playing with her food, not eating.

'Yes,' Rain said. 'Thanks, Grandma.' She meant it. There had been no time to think or worry. Everything bad was on hold. Only tomorrow it would all start again. No, not tomorrow. It was starting now.

'I want to talk to you about your father,' Grandma was saying. 'I know Max won't like it, but I think you have a right to know.'

'I don't understand,' Rain said. 'Know what?' The palms of her hands were sweating, and the prawn salad had turned to stone in her stomach.

'I kept in touch with him, you see. After you were born. After they split up. We liked him. He was a nice boy. He wanted to know about you, Rain. I don't care what Maxine said, I thought he had a right. You were his daughter. So I sent him pictures. Every time you came to visit me.'

Rain looked at the photographs in their silver frames on the dark, polished wood of the table at the side of the room. There she was, growing up: a tiny baby in a Rasta cardigan with stripes of green and red and yellow, and a tiny hat to match; one year old, holding herself upright against the settee, yelling with pleasure at something; throwing pieces of bread at some ducks, looking as if she wanted to run into the water. Rain could just about remember that. A picture for every year. And somewhere, her dad had looked at the same pictures.

'I've got others,' Grandma was saying. 'Other pictures of Cameron, and his wife, and his family.'

Rain felt as if someone had thumped her in the stomach. She could hardly breathe. Grandma went to the desk by the door and took out an envelope, then she sat down beside her. 'Here,' she said. 'This is Cameron's wedding. That's Becky. His wife.'

Rain hardly saw the pictures. One after another, Grandma passed them to her. She took them mechanically and held them in her hands. She saw children, three of them. Babies, then toddlers, then there was a picture of a girl, maybe a year or two younger than she was, and she felt a jolt of recognition.

'That's Julia,' said Grandma. 'I know. It's extraordinary, isn't it?'

Rain felt as if she was looking at herself. The girl looked just like her. The room was stuffy. Rain couldn't breathe. She felt as if the walls were closing in on her. 'Rain?' Grandma's face swam towards her through the thickened air.

'I'll be OK,' Rain said. She went into the hall and grabbed her coat. Then she opened the front door. The orange street lights shone through the fog. It was raw and cold, but at least she could breathe. Grandma called after her from the door: 'Rain? Where are you going?'

'A walk. Just round the block. I'll be fine.'

It was six o'clock. People were arriving home from work, cars pulling into driveways. She walked quickly along the pavement, looking in through the windows of the houses, catching glimpses of families eating their teas, watching TV. The smell of their meals floated on the cold air. Families. Suddenly, she had a family, too.

All her life, she'd looked at houses and families and schools from the outside, as if they were pictures on a TV screen, nothing to do with her. Now, she looked through the windows at the cosy scenes inside and thought, *My dad's out here somewhere, in a room like one of those, watching TV. Somewhere, there's a girl who looks like me.* But it still didn't seem real. This place didn't seem real. Little cubes of houses, neat hedges. This wasn't what she wanted.

Grandma was waiting in the doorway when she got back. 'Where have you been?' she said. 'I was just about to get the car out and come looking for you.'

'What am I going to do now?' demanded Rain. 'What will Max say?'

She didn't want *another* family. She only wanted Max. She wanted a windy night in a wild place in the bus and Max's arms warm around her. She should never have come here.

'You can meet him if you want,' said Grandma. 'He'd like that. I know you'd like him. You'd like all of them.'

'I don't *want* to meet them. Why did you have to tell me? All this time, you never said anything.'

'You wanted to know about him, dear. You said so.'

Rain felt she couldn't bear to be in Grandma's house a second longer. 'I want to go home,' she said.

'Don't be silly. You can't go now.'

'I'm going to pack. I have to go home, Grandma.'

She ran upstairs and threw her things into her bag. There were two carrier bags full of clothes Grandma had made her buy. She didn't want them. She didn't want anything except for everything to be normal again. When she came downstairs, Grandma had her coat on, and they drove through the rainy night.

'Just what I expected,' said Grandma when they arrived in Bells Green. 'The middle of nowhere. Where now?'

Rain pointed out the narrow gap between the overhanging bushes and Grandma edged the car between them, muttering about her paintwork. Light spilled across the garden from the curtainless windows, and for the first time, the cottage felt like home to Rain. She got out of the car and Leaf bounded towards her. 'Hi, Leaf,' she said. 'What are you doing here?' But as soon as she said it, she knew. She went in through the kitchen door and Max and Simon were there, on either side of the table, a bottle of wine open, the remains of a meal in front of them. Max started up from the table.

'Rain? I thought you were coming tomorrow.'

Before Rain could reply, Grandma was there. 'Rain was homesick,' she explained. 'So I brought her home early.'

'I . . . I'd better go,' Simon said. 'You have a good holiday, Rain?'

'Grandma told me all about my dad.' Rain heard the words coming out of her mouth as though someone else was speaking. 'She's got pictures. She knows him, Max. He's got a wife and a family. I've got a brother, Max, and two sisters.'

'Is this true?' Max had turned white. Rain nodded. 'How could you?' she said to Grandma. 'How could you do that without asking me? What have you done?'

'I did what I thought was right,' Grandma said defiantly. 'She had a right to know. Cameron had a right to know.'

'What? Know what?'

'I send him photos. I tell him how she's getting on. That's all. He has a right. He's her father.'

Simon hadn't left. He'd moved closer to Max. 'Calm down,' he said to her now. 'You're—'

'Don't you tell me what to do,' said Max,

turning on him. 'She's my mother and I'll tell her what I think of her if I want to.'

'Stop it!' cried Rain. 'All of you, just stop.' She fled, sobbing, up the stairs and threw herself on her bed. She heard the sound of Grandma's car pulling away, and then she heard voices, Simon's and Max's. Simon whistled to Leaf, and she heard his footsteps outside, then Max came up the stairs. Her door opened and she felt Max's weight on the bed beside her, then Max's hand, gentle on her back.

'I'm sorry,' Max said softly. 'I'm really sorry, Rain. I haven't been a lot of use, have I?'

Rain sat up, wiping her eyes. 'What am I going to do, Max?'

'What do you mean?'

'What am I going to do about my dad?' Max was silent. 'I wish I'd never asked you about him,' Rain continued. 'Then Grandma wouldn't have seen those photos and she wouldn't have told me anything.'

'Yeah, right.' Max's voice was suddenly harsh. 'She would have told you sooner or later, believe me. Imagine her keeping in touch with him all this time. She was just waiting for her chance.'

'But she didn't mean to upset anyone. She was trying to help.'

'You try living with her for seventeen years,' said Max, 'and then see what you think. I wouldn't live the life she wanted me to, I wouldn't be who she wanted me to be, but she's still trying to control me. I bet somewhere in her devious little mind she's still plotting for me to marry Cameron.'

'But she was kind to me, Max. She's always been kind to me. You know that.'

'That's different.' Max fell back into a moody silence.

'I thought you might know what to do,' Rain said at last. 'If I don't meet him, I'll never find out whether—'

'Meet him!' Max exploded. 'Who said anything about meeting him? No, don't answer that. Look, it's dead simple, Rain. You don't have to do *anything* you don't want to do.'

'But can't you see, I don't know what I want? If I never meet him, I'll always wonder, won't I, what it would have been like? I feel like there's something missing, Max, inside me. Maybe if I go and meet him I'll feel right again. Why won't you tell me what to do?'

'Because I can't,' Max said quietly. 'Because, if it was me, I don't know what I'd do. Because I can't see into the future. Because sometimes I feel as if I've made all the wrong choices all the way along the line and it seems as if it's all coming apart.'

Rain didn't know what to say. She reached out for Max in the darkness, and held her very tightly for a long time.

14

Rain woke in the morning to find Max lying on the bed beside her. She looked at Max's sleeping face and remembered the last time she'd woken like this, with Max. It had been in their tent, on a beach in Scotland in the summer. It seemed so long ago now, but it could only be a few months. She remembered with a shock the things Max had said the night before. She couldn't believe Max had said them. Max was always so certain, so definite, so confident.

Rain went to the window and looked out. All the leaves had gone now, except on the oak trees. They were always the last to get their leaves, and the last to lose them. The willows and ashes were all bare branches, and she could see between them, past the overgrown hedges of Simon's farm to the flat fields of his neighbours, and on into the distance.

'He's out there, somewhere.' She spoke her thought aloud without meaning to.

'He always was.' Rain turned from the window to see Max stretching and yawning. 'You just didn't know who he was. You didn't know how to find him. That's the only thing that's changed. I meant what I said last night. You don't have to do anything. Not until you want to. It really is up to you, whatever my mother says.'

Rain heard the sound of wheels on gravel outside and went back to the window. Simon appeared, pushing a wheelbarrow with a box balanced on top. Instantly a picture filled her mind of the scene when she'd arrived home the night before, Max and Simon having a cosy supper together. She felt as if everything was shifting around her, as if nothing was solid. 'It's Simon,' she said. 'Max, what's going on?'

'He's bringing some chickens,' said Max. 'Didn't you see the chicken run I built? And a little house. It's brilliant. I'll show you.'

'That's not what I meant,' Rain began. But Max had gone.

Simon was at the door with a clucking box in his arms when she went downstairs. 'Take a look,' he said to Rain. 'They're Rhode Island Reds. You like chickens, don't you? Max told me.'

Max was filling the kettle at the sink. 'It's OK,' Rain told Simon. 'I'm not bothered.'

She saw a look pass between Simon and Max. Then Simon said, 'Go on. They won't hurt you.' He lifted the lid and tilted the box towards her. She looked in spite of herself. The box was a sea of orangey brown feathers. A beady eye blinked at her, and there was a flurry of movement. Simon jammed the lid back on quickly, before they could escape. 'I've brought you three,' he said. 'We can go and catch a cockerel later. You can raise your own chicks. Shall we put them outside?'

'Go on,' said Max. 'I'll make some tea.'

Max had been busy in the garden. The chicken house was typical Max. It looked a bit like the Taj Mahal, with a little wooden tower on top.

'I know,' said Simon, when he saw her face. 'More like a palace, isn't it? Here, stick your hands inside and grab hold.'

Rain plunged her hands in through all the feathers, and there was a small, warm body in the middle of them. The chicken was silent as she lifted it from the box, but when she dropped it over the fence it exploded in a flurry of feathers and clucking. She dropped the other two in to join the first one, and very soon they were all pecking happily at the grass.

'That's all right then,' said Simon. He seemed nervous, suddenly.

'I . . . I'll go and see if the tea's ready,' Rain said.

She started to walk away, but Simon called her name, so she stopped. 'I think Max was trying to help you. You know, at school? She told me what happened.'

'You've been talking about me? While I was away? But it's nothing to do with you.'

'No, but—'

'I don't want to hear this.'

'OK. Look . . .'

Rain turned away.

'I'll go then,' Simon said. 'I'll see you later, OK?'

When Rain didn't reply, he walked past her, past the cottage and out through the trees. It was what she'd thought. Max and Simon. She felt sick. As if she hadn't got enough to worry about already. And she'd almost forgotten about school with everything else that had happened, but now Simon had reminded her about that, too.

A few minutes later, Max appeared with

three cups in her hand. 'Where's Simon?' she asked.

'He went home.'

'What did you say to him?'

For a second, Rain thought Max was going to be angry. She felt stupid and miserable, but she couldn't explain to Max.

'You'll just have to drink two cups, then,' Max said, and Rain knew she was upset and trying not to show it. 'Listen,' Max continued. 'I forgot to tell you, Daniel's coming round any time now. I went to his house while you were away. I saw his drawings. He's a talented kid.'

'You wouldn't think so if you saw him at school.'

'Maybe not. You don't mind me inviting him round?'

Rain shook her head. 'It's fine,' she said. 'Everything's fine.' She took her cup of tea and went up to her room.

Half an hour later the blue estate car arrived. Daniel's mum was driving, and Daniel was beside her in the front seat. When Rain went outside she was instantly surrounded by the girls.

'Where's your bus?' asked Kerry. 'Why isn't it here?'

'We don't live in it any more,' Rain told her. 'We live in the cottage now.'

'Oh.' All three looked disappointed.

'Maybe I'll show you later,' Rain said. She would have liked to visit the bus herself, but right now she didn't feel like bumping into Simon.

'We're going to see our dad,' Kerry announced.

'He's got a flat,' Annette said proudly. 'We can sleep there.'

'Not tonight,' Kerry added quickly. 'He hasn't got any beds yet.'

'Daniel didn't want to come,' said Annette.

'But I saw him,' Rain said. 'Where did he go?'

'In there,' said Kerry, pointing to the studio.

Max was standing by the car, talking to Daniel's mum. Rain went into the studio and stopped. Max had hung a painting on the wall at the side, a huge painting of mountains and sea and sky. It was Rain's favourite of all the paintings Max had ever done. She'd begged Max not to sell it, and she had reluctantly agreed, but Rain hadn't seen it since the day Max had stored it away under her bed in the bus. Daniel was staring at it, not moving.

'It's amazing,' he said. 'Where is that place?'

'Scotland. Way up in the north. It's light almost all night in the summer. And this time of year, when the storms come, and the big waves . . . You wouldn't believe it.'

Rain felt a sudden sense of loss. She'd given all that up. And for what?

'I want to know how she does that,' Daniel said, looking closely at the surface of the painting. 'I wouldn't know where to start.'

'You'd better ask her, then.'

'I will.' Daniel paused, then he said, 'I'm sorry about what happened at school. It was my fault.'

'What, your fault I hit Stephen? Come off it.'

'I should have done it myself. I wish I had.'

They stood for a moment, both of them looking at the painting.

'The girls told me about your dad,' Rain said. 'Is it true?'

'He's got a flat in Norwich. They all think it's a game. They don't understand.'

'Why don't you want to see him?'

'Are you kidding? It's because of me he left. How can I go and see him? And I don't want him to have a stupid flat. I want him to come home.'

'I'm sorry.' Rain felt useless. She didn't know what to say.

Daniel was still staring at the painting. After a while he turned to her. 'Your mum, Max, she came round to our house.'

'She told me.'

'She looked at my drawings. And you were right. She didn't laugh at them. Then she made me show them to Mum.'

'Yeah? What did *she* say?'

'She didn't want to be bothered at first, but Max made her look. And afterwards her and Max talked for a really long time. I think . . . I think it made Mum feel better.'

'What, looking at your pictures, or talking to Max.'

Rain meant it as a kind of joke, but Daniel was serious. 'Both,' he said. 'And then Max said I could come today and she'd, like, teach me. So here I am.'

Rain looked out of the open door to where Max and Daniel's mum were standing talking. Daniel's mum still looked unhappy, but something about her was different. 'Max persuaded Mum to take a bit of time off work,' Daniel said, as if he was reading her mind. 'She was doing too much. She couldn't keep it up. Not . . . not with everything else.'

Rain started to reply, but Daniel had turned to look at the picture of the marshes that filled the far wall of the studio. It was still red, but now there were black brush stokes and charcoal markings all over it. 'Why is it all red like that?' he asked.

'It's the earth,' said Max from the doorway. 'And the sunlight. The earth shows through the landscape. It's always there, underneath. And the sun's always there even if you can't see it. You see blue and grey when you look at the sky, but the other colours are there too. The red makes the painting come alive. Or that's what I hope, anyway.'

'This one,' said Daniel, looking at the painting of mountains and sea. 'Did you do this the same way?'

'More or less. Different colours, same idea. You're still interested, then?'

Daniel nodded, looking around the studio now for the first time, his gaze running over the bottles and jars, the pots of brushes and pens and pencils. Max had tidied up a bit, but there was still paper everywhere. Daniel wasn't staring at the mess though. He was staring at a drawing that was pinned to the wall. It was crumpled and torn, held together with tape. It was his drawing, the picture of Rain. She felt her face growing hot. Daniel walked closer and looked at it, then he turned back to them.

'Where did you get it? I thought . . .'

'I rescued it,' Rain said. She could feel Daniel staring at her.

'It's good,' Max told him.

'The thing is,' Daniel said slowly, glancing at Rain again, 'sometimes it works and sometimes it doesn't. And I don't know why.'

'You need hard work and a bit of help,' Max said. 'And I don't suppose you'll get the help at school. Look, here.' She moved quickly, setting up an easel and a drawing board. 'You draw me. I'll sit for you. Only do it quickly. Go on. You've got two minutes.' She thrust a piece of charcoal into Daniel's hand and sat down.

Rain expected Daniel to freeze. Max had tried this with her, in the days when she'd still hoped Rain might have the gift. Rain remembered the arguments. In the end, she'd simply refused to try. But Daniel started to draw. He worked fast, slashing lines onto the paper.

'Time's up,' said Max. 'Get a new bit of paper and do another one. Use one of those pens this time. Any one. Go on.'

'Aren't you going to look at what I've done?'

'Later,' said Max. 'Get on with it.'

'I'll go and see what everyone else is doing,' Rain said. Neither of them heard her. Max was staring into some inner distance and Daniel was working frantically. There was total concentration on his face. Rain went out into the garden. The girls were playing houses. Hayley was a dog and Annette was a baby. They were using the cardboard box the chickens had come in for a dog's basket.

'Mum's gone for a walk,' Kerry told Rain. 'You can be the daddy.'

'I . . . I don't really feel like it,' Rain said, looking back at the studio. Max and Daniel were bent over Daniel's drawings. She could feel the connection between the two of them. Something very strong. Something she couldn't share. Only this morning, when she'd woken up with Max beside her, she'd felt that everything was going to be all right. But now . . .

She'd never had to share Max with anyone before. Always it had been the two of them, together against the world. Now there was Simon, and Daniel too. And there was something else, a feeling she'd never had before, a kind of sick dread that had begun to build up inside her, colouring the way she felt about everything else. She realized now that it had been there all the time she had been with Grandma. It was still there now. The feeling had faces to go with it. Stephen, Stacey, Darren, Charlene, Mr Crawley. She hated admitting it, even to herself, but she didn't want to go back to school.

15

Rain watched the chickens and thought how simple their lives were. They looked completely happy, pecking around in the grass. She heard Daniel's mum calling to the girls, saying goodbye to Daniel. She heard the car drive away.

The girls had eaten all the bread, so Rain fetched the bread bowl and heated some water. She sprinkled in the yeast and the sugar and watched the yeast come alive and start to grow. It felt good, doing something simple, something useful. She could forget about everything while she was making bread. She was stirring flour into the mixture when Max put her head through the door and said, 'I'm going over to Simon's. He's got a sack of chicken pellets for us. You OK?'

Rain nodded, and Max was gone. She covered the bowl with a cloth and put it by the range for the dough to rise, then she went to find Daniel. He was sitting at the

179

table in the studio with a stack of Max's art books beside him. He looked up when Rain came in. 'I never knew there *were* things like this,' he said. 'They're all different, and they're all amazing. Gauguin.' He pointed at the book that lay open in front of him, patterns of brown bodies, coloured fabrics and vegetation. 'Cézanne, Picasso, Van Dyck. There's just so much. I could spend days looking at it.'

Rain knew how he felt. She felt the same way about these books, but they were so much a part of her childhood, part of *her*, that it was almost as if Daniel was looking at her secret diary. She knew it was stupid, but she couldn't help it. She couldn't keep the coldness out of her voice.

'Yeah, right.'

'Rain? What is it?'

She felt bad at once. She knew Daniel had been sharing something important with her, even if he hadn't meant to. And she'd just brushed it aside.

'Can I see your drawings?' she asked him.

Daniel stopped what he was doing. 'Most of them aren't much cop,' he said, but Rain could see the enthusiasm returning to his face. He shuffled through a huge stack of paper.

'Look,' he said finally. 'This one.'

Max's face stared up at Rain. Before she knew what was happening, there were tears in her eyes. She wiped them away quickly, but Daniel was looking at the picture, not at her. 'I think I caught something in this one,' he said. 'It feels pretty weird, though, just looking and looking at someone like that. After a while, their face seems to change. It's like you don't know them at all. What do you think?'

'It's good,' Rain said shakily. 'It's really good.' Daniel had drawn the real Max. It wasn't her *face* he'd drawn. It was something inside her. It was a feeling.

'She's brilliant, your mum,' Daniel was saying. 'She makes it all seem so easy. And she makes it seem like something important.' His eyes were shining.

'I'd better go and see to the bread,' she said, and left him poring over the books.

Later, when the bread was in the oven and Max had finally returned from Simon's, Mrs Moore arrived to collect Daniel. The girls were sleepy in the back of the car, but

Kerry wound the window down and said, 'You didn't show us the bus.'

'Maybe next time. How was your dad? Did you have fun?'

Kerry's face fell. 'It was boring,' she said.

Daniel appeared from the studio, clutching a sheaf of drawings. 'You've been busy,' said his mum, and Rain saw at once that she was trying hard to be cheerful for Daniel's sake. Daniel nodded, but the light had gone from his eyes. 'I'll see you Monday,' he said to Rain, as he got into the car.

Later still, when Rain was taking the bread out of the oven, she heard a weird warbling noise. The noise got louder and louder until Max, who'd been drawing at the kitchen table, suddenly jumped to her feet. 'It's the phone,' she exclaimed. 'Where is it?'

'What phone?'

But Max had located the phone in a pocket of her overalls and was trying to figure out which button to press. Rain watched, open-mouthed, as Max put the phone to her ear. 'Yes . . . Well, obviously it's working. Yeah, OK. You too.' She pressed another button and put the phone down on the table. Then she saw Rain's face. 'So? What are you staring at?'

'You. You hate telephones.'

'Yeah, well . . .' Max smiled to herself.

'Does this mean we can have all the other things on your blacklist now? Like oven chips and ice creams and sweets?'

'You have sweets sometimes,' said Max. 'And ice creams.'

'Where did you get the phone?'

'Simon gave it to me.'

Rain felt the heat of the loaf burning through the cloth she was holding it with. She put it down on the table.

'Max—'

But Max had already started to speak. 'I've been meaning to tell you. But you've been having such a hard time, and it never seemed like the right moment.'

'Tell me what?' Rain knew, but she had to hear Max say it.

'Me and Simon. You know I like him. We like each other. We—'

'Are you in love? Is that what you're saying?'

'No. I'm saying we're *friends*. I don't know. Maybe more than friends. Everything that's happened, it hasn't been easy for me either, you know. Simon's helped. You like him too, don't you?'

'We don't *need* anyone else. We were fine the way we were. Just the two of us.'

'Were we?' Max asked gently. 'Are you sure about that?'

And later, when they'd eaten, she said, 'Everything changes, Rain. Nothing stays the same for ever.' But they didn't talk about Simon again that night.

Rain spent Sunday doing homework. She hadn't even looked at her school bag since the day Max had dragged her from the school, but when she forced herself to look in her homework diary she found that there were several jobs she should have done. And now she remembered that she was going to be on report when she went back. That meant she had to be perfect, or she'd be in even more trouble. Max was helping Simon on the farm, but she had to not think about Max and Simon, because when she did she found herself drawing jagged black doodles in her exercise book. She'd already had to carefully remove one page. They didn't talk about Simon again that night either, and in the morning it was time for school.

'You're sure you're going to be all right?' asked Max at breakfast time. There had been a frost the night before, and this morning, for the first time, they were sitting indoors instead of outside by the fire. 'What about those kids who were causing the trouble?'

'It'll be OK,' Rain said. 'I can handle it.'

'Rain, I'm trying to help.'

'I told you, I don't need help.'

'That's why you look as if you're about to go to a funeral, then?' Rain didn't reply. 'OK. Have it your own way. But at least eat something before you go.'

Rain realized she'd been playing with her piece of toast. She didn't feel hungry, but she forced it down. Then she stood up, heaved her bag onto her back, and walked out to wait for the bus.

When they reached the village Daniel came and sat next to her. He'd never done that before. 'Are you OK?' he asked. 'Only, on Saturday when I left, I thought . . . You seemed a bit down.'

'What's up with everyone today?' Rain said. 'First Max, now you. I feel fine. I'm not worried about those creeps at school. I'm not worried about anything, all right?'

'I was only asking . . .'

'Well, don't.'

'Your mum,' said Daniel, tentatively.

'What about her?'

'She really helped me. I mean, she really knows what she's talking about. And it's fun. Like the way she tells you to do loads and loads of drawings. I mean, at school they'd just tell you not to waste paper. I did more yesterday afternoon, and the girls started drawing too, and Mum.'

'Well, that's great,' said Rain. 'I'm really pleased.'

Daniel looked at her, but didn't say anything, and Rain lapsed into silence. Then she looked out of the window and saw what had happened to the place where Tony Moore's garage had been. The garage had gone as if it had never existed. The site was a sea of mud and small rectangular islands of concrete floated in it – the shapes of houses. There were stacks of bricks and roof tiles and wood everywhere, and by the entrance there was a sign –

RURAL RETREATS
DESIGNING A DREAM
BUILDING A REALITY

'A nightmare, more like,' said Daniel.

Rain didn't reply. To her, it was all beginning to seem like a nightmare. Daniel took a book from his bag and started to turn the pages. She almost cried out when she saw what it was – a little book of drawings by famous artists that Max had given her, years ago, hoping that some of the magic would rub off on her. Somehow, her book must have got mixed up with Max's things, and now Daniel had it. She wanted to snatch it out of his hands, but instead she stared out of the window, not seeing anything, until they arrived at school.

Mrs Haynes asked Rain to wait behind after registration. She knew the rest of the class were all talking about her as they left. 'I'm sorry I have to do this, Rain,' Mrs Haynes began. 'I told Mrs Snowley the incident was quite out of character. You have to get this book signed by your teachers at the end of every lesson. It's not a big deal.'

Rain took the small red book. 'OK,' she said. 'Is that all?'

'You do know you can talk to me, don't you?' said Mrs Haynes. Rain couldn't bear the concerned look in her eyes. If she was going to get through this she was going to have to be tough, the way Max was tough when she faced up to people who tried to make them move on. The sympathy in Mrs Haynes's voice made her want to cry. She couldn't do that.

'I have to go,' she said. 'I mustn't be late, must I? Not now I'm on report.'

She picked up her bag and walked quickly from the room. Alice and Beth were waiting outside. 'We didn't think you'd come back,' Alice said.

Rain walked past her. She didn't want to talk to anyone. 'Hey, hold on,' called Beth. 'It was great what you did. It made Stephen look really stupid.'

'Leave me alone,' said Rain. 'That's all I want. Just leave me alone, all right?'

'OK,' Alice called after her. 'Be like that. We were trying to be friendly. We were trying to help.'

Rain walked away down the corridor, telling herself she didn't need them, she didn't need anyone. Then she opened the door of the history room, and all the faces turned towards her. 'You're late,' the teacher said.

'I . . . I'm sorry. I had to see Mrs Haynes.'

'Right. Sit down, then.'

Rain looked around. The only seat was next to Charlene. They were all watching her. She sat down and got out her books. Later, when she looked up, she saw Daniel trying to catch her eye, but she looked away again quickly, trying to concentrate on what the teacher was saying. But no matter how hard she tried, her mind kept veering away to other things, to Max and Simon, to her dad, and then back and away to the time when there was a bus and a wild place, and just her and Max together.

'Rain!' the teacher said sharply. 'I've asked you twice now. Have you been listening to a thing I've been saying?'

And at the end of the lesson, when she presented him with her report book, he said, 'I'm very disappointed, Rain. You'll have to do a lot better than this, I'm afraid.' He scribbled something in the book and then handed it back to her. She felt numb. She'd never actually been in trouble in a lesson before, not once. 'You'd better hurry,' said the teacher, 'or you'll be late again.'

Somehow, she kept a lid on her anger, walked from the room, and ran all the way to her English lesson. Mrs Haynes looked at her sharply when she came in, but after that she had her hands full with the jokers in the class. When the lesson was over, she picked up Rain's report book and glanced at the history teacher's comment. She was about to say something, but then changed her mind and signed the book herself.

Rain left the classroom. It was break time, and she saw Daniel hovering by one of the benches on the playground. She didn't want to talk to him. She was sick of people. Turning away from him, she walked off towards the far side of the field, to the place where she could catch a glimpse of the marshes, and imagine the distance beyond them, stretching away to the sea.

16

'Are you trying to avoid us, Rain?'

Rain turned, startled, and saw Stacey, Charlene and Marianne.

'We got in trouble because of you.'

'Oh yeah?' It was the first Rain had heard of it.

'Mrs Snowley had us in her office. But she couldn't do anything, because *we* hadn't done anything, had we?'

'That's right,' Marianne said. 'There's no law against *talking* to someone, is there? There's no rules about that. It's not as if we *hit* someone. Not like you did.'

Rain started walking back towards the school, trying to get away, but the three girls followed her. 'Don't you like being on report, then, Rain?' Stacey said.

'Is it a pain, Rain?'

'Your snooty mates don't want to know you now, do they?'

'Yeah,' said Charlene. 'You should have

heard what Alice said about you. I'll tell you, shall I, Rain?'

Rain told herself not to answer. Talking to them would only make it worse. In the end, she'd lose her temper, and she knew that was exactly what they wanted. She couldn't stop their words hurting though. She'd been upset when she'd argued with Alice and Beth. They'd only been trying to help, and now she'd made them into enemies.

'We all saw your mum,' Stacey was saying now. 'She looked like a total nutter. Can't she afford to buy proper clothes?'

They were all laughing. Rain reached the art room just in time. A second later and she would have cracked.

'Hey! Slow down,' said Mr Hogan as she crashed in through the door. Rain stopped. There was a funny smell in the room, and Mr Hogan was wearing a stripy apron and grinning. 'Welcome to the fish project,' he said, motioning Rain to a chair. There was a table in the middle of the room laid out like a fishmonger's slab, crushed ice and fish lying on top. 'For the rest of this term we will be living and breathing fish,' Mr Hogan said.

'You're not kidding,' someone muttered.

Mr Hogan pretended not to hear. 'Choose a fish, any fish,' he said. 'Take it away and do something with it. Draw it, paint it, make a collage. It's up to you. The materials are all there for you.'

Rain waited until everyone else had chosen, then picked up an orange spotted plaice and found an empty table. She sat there doing a very bad drawing, letting her anger and frustration die away. She looked exactly as Daniel had looked when she had seen him in that first art lesson, pale, tired, and a bit sad. Daniel wasn't like that now. Rain could see him working on the far side of the room, complete concentration on his face. She looked down at her own drawing; an oval blob with dots on. *Everyone can draw*, Max used to tell her, *you just have to loosen up a bit, that's all*.

'Not your strong point, is it?' Mr Hogan said as the bell went. Rain shook her head. 'Well, keep at it. You never know. One day inspiration might strike. It certainly has with Daniel. Have you still got that picture he did of you?' Rain nodded. Mr Hogan paused. 'I was sorry to hear you'd been in trouble,' he said. 'If there's anything I can do . . .'

They all know, Rain thought. *They're all talking about me. All the teachers, everyone.* She pushed the report book towards Mr Hogan. He looked at her for a moment, and then scrawled his name on the page. He watched her walk out of the room, then sighed and began to put the fish back into polythene bags.

Rain struggled through that day at school, and the next, and the next. It didn't get any better. She found herself doing exactly what she had told Daniel she would never do – keeping her head down, trying to make people not notice her, trying to blend into the background. At break times she looked for secret corners where she could be on her own. Sometimes it worked – the library was good, and the computer room on Thursday – but sometimes it didn't. Finding Rain became a game for Stacey and her friends. It was in the computer room that Daniel tracked her down.

'What are you doing?' he asked, looking over her shoulder at the screen.

'Leave me alone.'

'You can't keep hiding all the time. It's no good.'

'If they see me with you it'll just make it worse. They'll get bored in the end. Then they'll forget about me. I'm busy.'

Daniel stared at the jumble of numbers and diagrams on the screen. 'You are actually a genuine boffin, aren't you?' he said.

'What do you mean?'

'You're really interested in all that stuff. Maths, physics. The hard stuff.'

'I wouldn't be here if I wasn't. It's all useful. Well, most of it. It's no different from you and the drawing.'

'Of course it is. I hate maths – and science. You have to think too hard. And even then it's impossible to understand half of it.'

'Yeah, well, it's what I want to do, OK? It's what I'm good at. Now, are you going to let me get on with this or not?'

'Hey, look,' said Charlene, appearing in the doorway with her friends. 'Come and see what I've found.'

Rain flashed a look at Daniel. She didn't need to say anything. Daniel shrugged and walked out of the room without looking back.

*   *   *

The days turned into weeks. At home, Rain noticed that Simon kept out of her way. He stopped coming round in the evenings. Max said it was because she was busy with her painting, but Rain knew that they'd often been together during the day. She could read the signs: two plates left over from lunch time that Max had forgotten to wash up, the smell of Simon's aftershave in the house, Max's wellies outside the door covered in mud when she'd been helping Simon on the farm.

There was just one short moment each day when everything seemed normal. At night, after Rain had gone to bed, Max would come and sit beside her and talk about the work she had done on the painting that day. Rain would fall asleep listening to the sound of Max's voice, feeling her weight on the mattress beside her, feeling her hand stroking her hair. But then, much later, she would wake from dreaming to hear the muffled sound of Max's phone ringing, and then she'd hear Max's voice talking long into the night.

On Saturday afternoons, Daniel came to work with Max, and that was the most difficult thing of all. Max came to life when

Daniel arrived, and Rain couldn't stop herself feeling jealous. She managed to make herself say hello and goodbye to Daniel, and smile as if everything was fine, and then pretended to have homework to do, and hid in her room all afternoon. Not that Daniel and Max would have noticed, even if she'd been in the studio watching everything they did. Even when they came inside for a cup of tea before Daniel left, he would still be talking away, asking questions, eyes shining, cheeks red with excitement.

It was the end of November now. The days were short and cold. It was dark when Rain left for school in the mornings, and dark when she returned at night. She felt as if the days had been stolen from her, and found herself thinking more and more of their old life in the bus.

'We need to talk,' said Max, on a Saturday morning when breakfast was over. Rain had slept badly and woken late.

'What about?' asked Rain sullenly.

'About you being miserable. You can't go on like this, Rain. You know you can't.'

'I'm OK. I'm fine.'

'Oh, come on!' Max was suddenly angry. 'I

know how you feel about me and Simon. And I know you must be worrying about your dad. I'm doing everything I can not to make it hard for you, but how can I help you if you won't even talk to me?'

'You mean you'd stop seeing Simon if I asked you?'

'It's not like that.'

'Well, what's the point in talking if nothing I say will make any difference?'

Max was silent for a few moments. Then she said, 'What about your dad? Have you decided yet? Do you want me to ring Mum and arrange for you to meet him?'

'No!'

'Well, what about school, then? Is everything all right there?'

Rain saw her school bag leaning against the wall. She picked it up and grabbed a handful of books. 'Look,' she said, opening one. She had never let her work slip, not once. It was the one thing she had to hold onto. *Very good. Excellent work, Rain. V. neat.* It's all fine.' She closed the book again before Max could speak. 'I don't know why you're asking,' she said. 'You don't care about school anyway, do you?'

'I'm *worried* about you,' said Max. 'You're

bottling things up, and sooner or later it's all going to come out. Believe me, I know.'

Rain stood up. A confusion of feelings welled up inside her. What was the point of being good at science and maths anyway, when she couldn't tell Max about the thoughts that had begun to haunt her, not just in her dreams, but during the day, too? Pictures of Max and Simon together, of Simon always present, here in the house, here when she woke up in the morning, here when she went to bed at night. Sometimes she even found herself imagining his face bending down over hers, kissing her good-night the way Max did, the way a father might, and when that happened in the night, she woke up sweating and terrified. 'I'll feed the chickens,' she said, grabbing the pan of hot mash from the stove and going out into the garden before Max could say any more.

She emptied the mash into the round iron feeding bowl that Simon had given them. There was a layer of ice on the water bowl, so she broke it, and as she poured in fresh water she heard Daniel's voice. 'Hi! Any eggs yet?'

Daniel was pushing a rusty bike over the gravel. It was making a noise like a cheese grater rubbing on a brick. 'There's something wrong with it,' he said. 'I had to walk most of the way.'

'You're early.'

'Yeah, well, Mum and the girls have gone to visit Dad, so I thought I might as well come over here. Well, have they then?'

'What?'

'Laid any eggs.'

The hens had been in their new home for weeks now, but they still hadn't produced any eggs. Rain liked the chickens and she had taken over the job of looking after them, but she was starting to think that this was one more thing she was messing up. She lifted the wooden flap at the back of the hen house expecting to see nothing as usual, and was startled by a chicken clucking madly and flapping off the nesting box. And there was an egg. It seemed like a miracle. Rain picked it up. It was deep, golden brown. 'It's warm,' she said, amazed. 'Here, feel it.'

Daniel dumped his bike in the grass and took the egg from her hands. Their fingers touched for a second. 'That's incredible,' he said. 'I've never felt one warm like this before. I didn't know.'

'Me neither,' Rain said.

Rain looked at Daniel. He had changed so much since the first time she'd seen him. Mostly, she thought, he didn't look tired. She could still picture him with his hands in the washing-up bowl, in the middle of all that crazy confusion in his house, trying to look after his three sisters, telling her he was no good at anything. Well, he'd certainly found something he was good at. He seemed more solid somehow. And it was amazing how people left him alone at school these days. He'd even started to make friends. Rain realized she was staring. Daniel was holding the egg out to her. 'My dad rang last night,' he said.

'Yeah? Is he OK?'

'He's got a job. In a garage. He'll be able to give Mum some money, so when she goes back to work she won't have to do all that overtime.'

'So, it's good news then?' He didn't *look* as if it was good news, Rain thought.

'He wants to see me. He says he wants to *talk*.'

'And . . .?'

'He wants to take me to a football match. Norwich City. He used to take me before . . . before everything went bad.'

'So you don't want to go?'

'I don't want to see his stupid flat. He's my dad. He should be at home. I want him to come back. Kerry was going on about how she's going to have two beds, like that was *good*. I won't sleep at his flat. Not ever.'

Rain looked at him. 'But you will have to see him, won't you?' she said. 'Sooner or later you will.'

He hesitated. 'Would you come with me?'

Rain was silent. She looked down at the chickens, contentedly eating. 'You wouldn't want me there,' she said. 'Your *dad* wouldn't want me there.'

'He likes you. He asks about you. He calls you girl mechanic. It'd make it seem . . . more normal if you came too.'

'I don't know.'

'Hey, Daniel!' It was Max calling from the doorway of the cottage. A smile creased her face. 'You're early.'

'I've been drawing,' he said, unstrapping a roll of paper from a rusty rack on the back of the bike. Rain felt forgotten, abandoned. All of her earlier misery came flooding back.

'Great!' Max said to Daniel. 'Come in the studio and show me.'

As Rain watched them walk off together she felt something crack, something warm running over her fingers. The beautiful brown egg was crushed in her hand, bright yellow yolk dripping on the soggy leaves under her feet. She hadn't even shown it to Max.

She went inside and washed her hands. Her books were still lying on the table where she had left them, but now the thought of spending a whole day pretending to do homework seemed impossible. She put on her coat and scribbled a note to say that she had gone for a walk.

She stood by the pond and everything around her seemed colourless, the cold grey sky, the black and brown skeletons of the trees, even the grass seemed to have had the colour washed out of it by the November rain. With a shiver, she turned to walk past Simon's farm. Then she thought of the bus. She could see Simon, a black shape on his old grey tractor several fields away. He wouldn't be back for ages.

She walked through the yard. It was swept clean now and she could see where many of the buildings had been repaired. Then she pulled the barn door open and saw the bus. It seemed to have shrunk, but the paintings that covered its sides were as bright as ever. It felt like home, and Rain was crying as she opened the door and climbed inside.

It was dark inside the bus. It smelt sweet and musty, a smell of summer stored up. As Rain's eyes grew accustomed to the dim light she saw that Simon had stacked bales of hay at the back. She sniffed. There were other smells too, hiding under the smell of the hay, smells of linseed oil and turpentine, of resin and beeswax, the smells Rain had grown up with.

Halfway down the bus she could just make out the patterns of paint on the wall where her room had been. She sat down on a hay bale and leant back against the others that were stacked behind. When she closed her eyes the smell of the hay carried her back to the summer. She'd been helping an old crofter called Donald MacDonald put his hay to dry in stooks in his tiny field that looked out over islands and sea. The bus was parked down by the deserted beach, and Max was there, painting . . .

She woke up suddenly to feel a wet

205

tongue licking her hand. Leaf dumped himself on the floor beside her and started to scratch. 'Max?' called Simon. 'Is that you?'

Rain blinked and rubbed her eyes. For a second she had no idea where she was. Leaf, the smell of hay, the darkness . . . Then she remembered, and at the same time a light went on in the barn and she saw Simon's head appear in the entrance of the bus. 'Max?' Simon said again. 'Oh, it's you, Rain.'

'I can come here if I want, can't I?' Rain stood up.

'Yeah, sure. I'm sorry if I startled you. I thought you were Max. She . . . she comes here sometimes. She sits there, just like you were.'

'But why . . . ?'

'The same reason you do, I suppose. She misses it. The bus. The life. Well, bits of the life anyway. It wasn't all good times though, was it?' Simon paused, and looked at her. Rain shook her head.

'You're always going to miss things,' Simon went on. 'I miss London. I miss my friends, and cinemas, and going down the pub to see a band whenever I want. On a day like this, stuck out in the fields on a

206

tractor in the rain, I start thinking about going back there.'

Rain didn't say anything. There was a part of her that wanted to tell him, 'Well, why don't you then?' But Simon was still talking.

'. . . and then I think what would happen to this place if I let one of those big farmers get hold of it, and I think about what it could be like here if I keep working, and I think about all the good things that have happened lately . . .'

Rain knew he was going to start talking about Max. It was too much. 'I've got to go,' she said. 'Max won't know where I am.' She brushed past Simon and jumped out of the bus.

'You can come here any time,' Simon called after her. 'You don't have to sit in the dark. The light switch is by the door.'

Rain arrived home as Daniel was leaving. She still felt shaken by her meeting with Simon. She couldn't make sense of her feelings. The trouble was, she *liked* Simon. The things he said made sense. He was kind. He cared about plants and animals – and he knew a lot about them, too. Sometimes there were things she would have liked to ask him about, like the time last week when she'd had to revise for a science test. She hadn't been able to remember about osmosis and she'd been sure Simon would have known the answer. But she couldn't make herself ask him. She just couldn't.

And now she thought of Max sitting in the bus, just as she had done – Max, who always said, 'Never look back.' She'd never once told Rain she missed their life on the road. They had always told each other everything. Or then again, maybe they hadn't.

'I think I'm going to have to push it,' Daniel said.

'What?'

'You were miles away,' said Daniel. 'My bike. It's useless.'

Rain looked at the bike. This was something that did make sense. 'Let's have a look,' she said, taking the bike and up-ending it expertly. 'The mudguard's loose,' she told Daniel. 'The chain's rusty and it feels like your wheel bearings are in a bit of a state. I'll get some tools.'

It didn't take long to get the bike working. 'You should look after it better,' she said. 'Give it some oil once in a while. You should really strip those gears down completely if you want to get them properly clean.'

Daniel took the bike from her. 'You sound like my dad. I'd only mess it up. I'm about as good with a spanner as you are with a paintbrush. It's like we've got the wrong parents. Maybe we were mixed up at birth.'

'I don't think so,' said Rain. She'd enjoyed the feel of the tools in her hands again. She really should sort the van out. She looked at Daniel and remembered what he had asked her. At least going to a football match would be something different. 'I've been thinking,' she said. 'Do you still want me to go with you to see your dad?'

Tony was waiting for them at the bus station. Rain saw him as the bus pulled in, looking nervously at his watch, and for a moment she wished she hadn't come. But then she saw the way his face lit up when he saw Daniel, and she knew she'd done the right thing.

'All right, Rain?' he said, putting a hand on Daniel's shoulder. 'How's that van of yours?'

'I haven't actually started on it yet. I . . . I haven't had time.'

'Oh, well,' Tony said. He looked at his

watch again. 'We'd better get moving, or we'll miss the kick-off.'

They followed the crowds of football fans through the city streets to the football ground by the river, and climbed to their seats high in the top tier of the stand.

Tony talked non-stop. About the team, about the manager's tactics and the things he was doing wrong, about the quality of the meat pies. Even when the game started, he didn't let up. He yelled advice to the referee and the linesmen and the players. Then Norwich scored and everyone was out of their seat, dancing, shouting, waving their arms in the air. And somehow, Rain was one of them. She didn't care about the football, but the huge blast of excitement and celebration swept her away. She could see why people came.

'You enjoyed it, then?' said Tony as they waited at the bus stop afterwards.

'Thanks,' Rain said. 'I had a really good time.'

Tony ruffled Daniel's hair. 'We'll do it again, then, yeah?'

Daniel smiled and nodded. He'd been smiling most of the afternoon. But when they were on the bus, and they'd seen Tony walking away among the crowds, he was quiet.

'It's a start,' Rain told him. 'And it was fun. We'll do it again, won't we?'

Daniel looked at her. 'I just want him to come home,' he said.

It was December now, and there were Christmas trees in all the houses. Rain stared in through the windows as the school bus made its way through the outskirts of the town on a Friday morning. Several houses had strings of lights in their gardens too, and one bungalow was dwarfed by a giant illuminated Santa Claus complete with sleigh and eight reindeer. Max didn't believe in Christmas, and Rain couldn't imagine them ever doing all this stuff. They celebrated the winter solstice instead, the moment in the year when the days stopped growing shorter; the moment the winter night was at its longest. Last year they'd been in Scotland. A huge fire of driftwood on the beach, and a big meal afterwards as the gales battered the bus. The solstice mattered to Rain because she knew it was real. Day, night, the earth turning – those were the things that made sense to her.

Unlike Santa Claus, she thought, as another set of flashing Christmas lights came into view outside the misted-up window. She began to prepare herself for the ordeal of school.

It was the final day of the fish project. Rain had accumulated a number of blobby drawings and a collage of material and sequins. It looked to her like something a five-year-old might have done. Daniel's sisters could have done it better. 'Right, then,' Mr Hogan said. 'I'd like you to lay out your work so we can all take a look. Use the walls too, if you want.'

Rain didn't need to use the walls. Neither did quite a few other people. She glanced around the room and was relieved to see that her work was no better or worse than anyone else's – apart from Daniel's.

Daniel seemed to have done far more work that he could possibly display. Mr Hogan went over to him and started leafing through the pile of drawings, pausing every so often to inspect one more closely. Gradually, everyone in the room stopped what they were doing and watched him. Rain was certain they all thought Daniel was going to be in deep trouble. He was wasting paper, wasn't he? Mr Hogan cleared his throat and Daniel looked up. 'These are terrific, Daniel,' Mr Hogan said. 'Take a look, everyone. Here, Daniel, grab the other end.'

Together, they pinned the drawing to the wall. Daniel had taped four sheets of paper together to do it. The fish was at least ten times life size. It had an eye the size of a fried egg.

'That's a whale,' said someone, but nobody laughed. Rain looked at their faces, and saw that they were all impressed. Daniel just stood there. He didn't seem bothered.

Mr Hogan put the drawing down and picked up a different one. 'Where did you learn to do this?' he asked.

'Well . . .' Too late, Rain realized what was coming. 'It's Rain's mum, Max,' Daniel said. 'She's an artist. A real one. She's been helping me.'

And now they were all looking at Rain. Mr Hogan muttered something to himself. He crossed the room and started rummaging through an untidy bookshelf before grabbing a large white book. He laid it on his table, still muttering, before picking up the book and working his way back across the room towards Rain. He put the book on her desk, covering up her stupid, blobby fish. There, on the left-hand page, were two of Max's paintings. Rain couldn't work out what he was showing her, or why. 'Is this your mum?' he demanded.

'What *is* this?' she asked him.

'Max Smith,' he said. 'She *is* your mum, isn't she?' He was almost shaking with excitement.

'These are her pictures,' Rain told him, 'but I don't understand.'

'It was a big show,' Mr Hogan said. 'Two years ago at the Reddy Gallery. Modern landscapes. This is the catalogue.'

Rain started reading the notes in the book. Words swam into focus and out again. *Reclusive landscape artist, Max Smith . . . never given an interview . . . refuses to talk about her work . . .* Her mind flashed back to their last drive through the crowded London streets, Max grumbling about the traffic, the pollution, edging the bus into a narrow entry in a side street. Rain remembered the man with floppy blond hair and narrow, rimless glasses who had come to the back door and helped them carry the paintings into the empty gallery. They might have been delivering boxes of fish, Rain thought. Max wouldn't even wait while the man looked at the paintings. She wouldn't even stop for a cup of tea. Rain looked back at the catalogue . . . *big canvases full of light and movement . . . surely this year Smith will be nominated for the Turner Prize . . .*

'I don't suppose . . .' Mr Hogan was saying, 'I mean . . . you don't think she'd come in and talk to everyone? It would be amazing.'

Rain couldn't speak. Max should have told her. And as for Max coming into school, talking to this lot . . .

'I'll ask her,' Daniel said.

They started on her at lunch time, in the cafeteria. Most of the tables were already full when Rain arrived, so she sat down on her own and started eating her lunch. Suddenly, she was surrounded. The usual bunch, Stacey, Charlene, Marianne. And Stephen hovering behind them with his mates to see what happened. At first they just stared. Rain ignored them and carried on eating.

'What's it like then, in your bus? Where do you go to the toilet?'

They all sniggered.

'I don't live in a bus. Not any more.'

'But you used to, didn't you? What did you do? Dig a hole in the ground?'

'Is that right, then? Your mum paints pictures?'

'We all thought she was a bus driver.'

It was so stupid. Rain still couldn't believe it was so upsetting. If only Daniel had kept his mouth shut. It had been better this week. Some days, they'd almost forgotten about her completely. They were laughing now. Rain forced herself to take another bite of her sandwich. She'd made the bread the night before, but it tasted like sawdust.

'What kind of bread's that?' one of them said.

'Gippo bread,' said someone else.

'I made it myself,' Rain told them.

'That's what I said. Gippo bread.'

They're like midges, thought Rain, the ones you get in Scotland. You think they can't hurt you. They're only tiny after all, and each bite is tiny, too, not like a wasp sting, but they keep on and on until you can't stand it any more. She stood up and her chair clattered to the floor, but before she could move, Daniel was there, standing in front of Stephen.

'Just leave her alone, OK?' he said. His hands were fists at his sides. His knuckles were white.

'*Ooooooh.*'

'It's true love,' said Marianne, 'I knew it.'

'Shut up,' said Daniel. 'You've caused enough trouble already.'

'That's funny,' said Stephen. 'I thought it was Rain who caused the trouble. I thought it was Rain who got suspended. Pretty pathetic though, isn't it, getting your girlfriend to do your fighting for you? You're useless, aren't you?'

'Leave it, Daniel,' Rain said. She jammed her lunchbox into her bag and walked towards him, trying to get out. She saw people standing up on other tables and a couple of dinner ladies ran out of the room. A crowd was gathering around them.

'How's your *dad*, then, Daniel? We've got new kit now, you know. See, we didn't want a *loser* as a sponsor, did we?'

Rain had forgotten about the football. It seemed so long ago. Then, too late, she saw what Daniel was going to do. He dropped his bag and swung his fist at Stephen.

'Daniel, *no*!' Rain stepped in front of him and the side of her head exploded in pain. She staggered backwards and heard Stephen's voice.

'Nice one, Daniel,' he jeered. 'Beating up your gippo girlfriend. Pathetic.'

Rain turned on him. She'd always thought seeing stars was just something people said, but she could see them now, swimming across her vision. Before she could say anything, she heard Mr Crawley's voice. He was pushing his way through the crowd. 'I might have known. Wherever there's trouble, you seem to be right in the middle of it, young lady. I think you'd better come with me.'

18

'But it wasn't her,' said Daniel. 'It was me.'

'Oh yes? Daniel Moore, isn't it? I seem to have heard your name before too. You'd better join us.'

Rain's head was clearing and she was angry. She felt as if she had been living in a very bad dream and she had suddenly woken up. She'd spent weeks trying to make herself invisible and it hadn't made any difference. She might as well have come to school the way she had on that very first morning, with all her earrings and her ragged jeans . . . They didn't *want* her to fit in. They didn't *want* her at all.

'Why don't you like me?' she said.

She didn't know if she was saying it to Mr Crawley, or to all of them – the words just came out. And they stopped Mr Crawley dead. Everyone was looking at Rain, and she didn't care.

'You want to know what it's like, living in a bus?' she said to Stacey. 'Well, I'll tell you.

You find some nice place to park up, out of everyone's way. Somewhere no one ever goes. And you're there for a day or two, not hurting anyone, and then someone comes. Maybe a farmer, maybe someone from the parish council, maybe a couple of policemen in a car. And they come and they bang on the side of the bus and they might be polite, if you're lucky. Or they might be rude, but the message is the same. *We don't want you here.* And you can live with that, only there's more. There's people who come in their cars and they're drunk and it's the middle of the night and they yell, and bang on the bus and that's *scary* because you know that you're on your own and then a brick comes through the window and you just want to know why they hate you so much. And I thought it would be different here. Only it's not, is it?'

She was shaking. Suddenly there was nothing left to say. She felt someone's hand on her shoulder and realized it was Mrs Snowley. 'What's been going on here, Mr Crawley?' she said.

'I . . . er . . .' He coughed, looked around at the watching faces. 'It's nothing. A minor incident. All dealt with.'

220

'No it's not.' It was a girl's voice, from the back of the crowd. Alice pushed her way to the front. 'It wasn't Rain's fault at all. They were . . . they were . . .'

'Yes?'

'They were going on at her. Stupid questions. Trying to wind her up. And Daniel tried to stop them and then Stephen . . . Well . . . he *deserved* to get thumped.'

There was a murmur of agreement from the back of the crowd. Mrs Snowley looked at Stephen. He looked away. 'I don't understand,' she said. 'It seems to be Rain who has been thumped, as you so nicely put it. But I don't want to discuss it here. I'll see you all in my office in fifteen minutes. Rain, you come with me and we'll get that head seen to.'

'I don't think so,' said Rain.

'Wait,' said Mrs Snowley. 'Where are you going?'

'Anywhere,' said Rain. 'Out of here. I've had enough.'

'But you can't . . .'

Rain ran from the cafeteria. She ran down the corridors, out through the front entrance of the school, across the car park, and out of the gates. She stood on the pavement and took a long, deep breath. It felt like the first proper air she had breathed in weeks, fresh, clean, cold. It felt like freedom.

She started to walk but she had no idea where she was going. She walked fast at first, past the playing field and down the lane that led to the marshes, but gradually she slowed, and then she heard the sound of running feet behind her, and Daniel's voice. 'Rain, wait!'

She stopped. Daniel stood beside her, gasping for breath. 'What do you want?' she said.

'You have to come back,' said Daniel.

'No, I don't.'

'You're giving in,' Daniel said. 'The way I did.'

'It's not the same. I've seen sense, that's all. Nobody wants me there. Either they hate me or they couldn't care less. I don't *need* school. I'll join a library. I'll get Max to buy me a computer.'

'It's not true. People do care. You just won't see it, that's all. You hide away in corners and won't let anyone help you. You even hide when I come round to your house.'

'I don't.'

222

'Yes, you do. You know you do.'

Rain couldn't look at Daniel. She stared out over the marshes towards the sea. 'I fixed your bike, didn't I? I came with you to see your dad.'

'You know what I mean.'

'Yeah, well, maybe you should think what it's like for me,' Rain said angrily. 'I see you and Max out in the studio, doing things together. You're sharing something. It used to be like that when she was teaching me to read. When we did things to the bus. But it's all gone. And it's even worse when she's with Simon.'

Rain shivered. The wind was biting through her clothes. A path led from where they were standing down onto the marshes towards the river. She started to walk.

'Don't go,' said Daniel.

Rain paused. 'I'll freeze if I stand here any longer.'

'We ought to go back.'

'I told you, I'm not going back. You do what you like.'

Rain walked on and Daniel followed her down the path, slithering on the mud. 'You *wanted* Max to help me,' he called after her. 'You saved that drawing from the bin.'

'That was before.'

Rain walked on in silence until she reached the river bank. The river was wide and muddy, swirling between beds of pale brown reeds. She turned and saw Daniel struggling along the muddy path behind her.

'You're pig-headed and you're stupid,' he said, when he finally stood beside her on the bank. 'Your mum, she's brilliant, but you just make her miserable. People try to help you at school, but you won't let them . . .'

'Oh yeah? Like who, exactly?'

'Like Alice, and Beth. Like me. And other people, too. Didn't you see their faces, in the cafeteria? What you said – it was true, and they knew it was.'

But Rain was thinking about the other thing Daniel had said. 'What do you mean, Max is miserable?'

'You haven't even noticed, have you? Max and Simon . . .'

'What about them?'

'Oh, come on. You must be able to see. She really cares about him. And Simon . . . well, you won't even give it a chance. Mum and Dad were like that, when I was little.

Always holding hands. Hugging each other. You don't know how lucky you are.'

'They don't do that!' The words came out as a wail, but Rain knew as she said them that it must be true. She'd been trying to pretend that it wasn't, but it was.

'Why is it such a bad thing?' Daniel said.

'I'm not ready. Can't you see? I haven't even met my *real* dad yet. I'm not ready for *another* one. I want it to be just me and Max. I want it to be how it was before.'

'But it can't be, can it?'

Rain gazed into the river. She looked into the swirling water for a long time without speaking.

'Please,' said Daniel at last. 'Come back to school. It . . . it wouldn't be the same without you.'

Rain looked at him. 'What do you mean?'

'I thought we were friends. I'd miss you if you weren't there.'

Tears stung Rain's eyes and she looked away. The marshes and the sky blurred together. 'I'm going back,' Daniel said, and he turned and began to walk away. 'You do what you like.'

Rain saw him slipping and squelching clumsily along the path away from her. She felt that if she let him go it would be the end. She didn't want it to be like that. 'Wait,' she called after him. 'Daniel! Wait for me. I'm coming.'

When they finally stood on the road again they looked at each other. Their shoes were covered in mud. Both of them had mud splashed up their legs. 'You're a mess,' said Rain.

'You too.' Daniel tried to rub some of the mud from his trousers, but that only made it worse. He stood up and looked at Rain. 'You're going to do it then? You're coming back?'

Rain didn't say anything. She started walking towards the school, but the closer they got, the heavier her legs felt. How *could* she go back there after what had happened? It wasn't just today. There would be weeks, and months, and years. She remembered the thrill she'd felt only an hour ago when she had come running out of the school, the way the air had tasted, the freedom. She stopped.

'What is it?' said Daniel. But before Rain could answer, she saw Simon's car coming towards them. It stopped beside them and Max jumped out. 'What's happening, Rain?

What's been going on? I got a phone call from the school. Why aren't you there?'

'I can't go back, Max,' Rain said miserably. 'I want to, but I can't do it.'

'Hey,' said Max gently, pulling Rain towards her, holding her. 'Hey, what is this? You don't have to do anything you don't want. You know that.'

Rain stood back, wiping her eyes. 'I told you,' she said. 'I do want to. It's just . . . I don't think I can.'

Max looked at Daniel. 'Tell me,' she said.

'People at school have been picking on Rain,' said Daniel. 'They're idiots, and it seems, well, stupid, what they do. You wouldn't think it would matter, but it does. I should know.'

'And you let it happen? Didn't you tell someone? You should have told *me*.'

Daniel started to reply, but Max cut him off. 'Get in, both of you,' she said grimly. 'I'm going to sort this out once and for all. What are *you* doing?' she snapped at Simon, who had got out of the car.

'Just hold on a minute,' said Simon. Rain couldn't believe he'd said it. She waited for Max to hit the roof, but Max just stood there. 'Daniel, I think you'd better go back

227

to school,' Simon went on. 'Tell them Rain's with her mum, OK? We've got some things to talk about here.'

Daniel nodded. 'I'll see you later,' he said to Rain. She watched him go.

There was an odd look on Simon's face as he stood beside Max, as if he'd made up his mind to do something and no one was going to stop him. 'Why don't you tell us what's been happening?' he said.

Us, thought Rain. He said *us*. She saw Max look at Simon again, and suddenly she *knew*. There was no pretending any more. Max and Simon was a real thing. It wasn't something she could *stop*. Simon was going to be part of her life, whether she liked it or not. She was shivering again.

'Come on,' said Simon. 'Let's get in the car before we all freeze to death.'

Max sat in the back with her arm around Rain's shoulders, and Rain told them, right from the beginning, what it had been like at school. A couple of times she felt Max stiffen with anger, but she didn't interrupt, and now Rain found herself telling them about the scene in the cafeteria. 'You were right about school,' she said to Max. 'You were right all the time. I thought I could handle it, but I couldn't. And then I told them all what I thought of them.'

'You should have told *me*,' said Max.

'But . . . but I couldn't. It was because of you . . . you and Simon, because of Daniel, because of my dad. It was all mixed up inside me, Max. I thought I was on my own.'

'Well, you're not,' said Max. 'I don't know why we're sitting here. We should go straight in and sort things out. There's nothing complicated about it.'

'Max, it doesn't work like that. Look what happened last time.'

'OK, OK, so what do you want me to do?' Max was getting angry again. 'You want to go back. That's what you said.'

'How about *I* talk to them?' Simon said hesitantly. 'I could come in with you, Rain. That would be all right, wouldn't it?'

There was a silence. Max didn't appear to have heard Simon.

'I *do* want you to come with me, Max,' Rain said, 'but I don't—'

'What?' demanded Max.

'You *agreed* I could go to school,' said Rain. 'But all the time you go on about it. You know what I mean, grumbling about the uniform and the homework. And when

I need you to help, you act as if they're out to get *you*, not me. I don't need you to fight for me, Max. I just need you to be there.'

'Oh, right. So I go into that place with you and just sit there like a . . . like a jellyfish while they accuse you of things you haven't done . . . while they . . .'

'We don't know that,' said Simon.

'Who asked *you*?'

But Max's anger seemed to have no effect on Simon. 'Rain's right,' he insisted. 'You should be with her. And if you like, I'll come too. Then, when you start to get out of order, I can make you shut up, can't I?'

Rain stared at him. Somehow, she'd never thought of Simon as tough before. He'd always just seemed friendly, ordinary. Only she should have seen. Of course she should. Nobody stuck around Max if they weren't tough.

Max and Simon were looking at each other and Rain felt as though there was a conversation going on that she couldn't hear. Then suddenly it was over, and before she knew quite what had happened, she was walking through the school gates with Max beside her, and Simon following a little way behind them.

19

The school secretary showed them into Mrs Snowley's office. Mrs Haynes was there, too. 'I don't think we've met,' Mrs Snowley said, looking from Max to Simon.

'Simon's a friend,' said Max. 'There's no reason why he shouldn't be here, is there?'

'It's absolutely fine,' Mrs Snowley said. 'Please, have a seat.'

Max sat on the edge of a chair, and Mrs Snowley cleared her throat. 'I want to say right away that there have been some things going on in this school that I'm not very proud of. I'm not going to defend anybody or make any excuses. But I do want to try and make sure that this doesn't happen again.'

'I don't see how,' Rain burst out. 'It's just the way people are, isn't it? How are you going to change them? They always gang up and pick on anyone who's different.' This wasn't what she'd meant to happen, but she couldn't stop herself. 'Max was right. We were better off having nothing to do with any of it. We were better off on our own.'

'So why did you come back?' asked Mrs Snowley gently.

'I . . .' Rain felt herself reddening, thinking suddenly of Daniel.

'You're right, of course,' Mrs Snowley said. 'There are always going to be bullies. And even teachers can get things wrong sometimes. But that doesn't mean we can't try to make things better. Mrs Haynes has a suggestion to make . . .'

'Well?' Max said when they arrived home from the school and Simon had left.

'Well, what?' Rain felt exhausted, but there was something she had to ask Max. She'd been thinking about it all the way home.

'You didn't say a word in the car. You didn't say a lot to Mrs Snowley, either. What did you think of what they said?'

'I don't know.'

'Well, I thought it was a good idea. I thought Mrs Snowley talked sense. And that Mrs Haynes seemed OK, too.'

Rain looked up in surprise. It was the first time she'd heard Max say anything good about the school. About any school. 'Don't look so shocked,' Max said. 'If you and Daniel can help other kids, that's a good thing, isn't it?'

Rain nodded. Once she'd been sure that Mrs Snowley wasn't angry with her, that Max wasn't going to lose her temper, everything else Mrs Snowley had said had been a kind of blur. Then Mrs Haynes had explained what they were going to do. She wanted Rain and Daniel and some of the others to have some kind of training. If people were in trouble they'd be there for them to talk to. Mrs Haynes was going to help. Rain had tried to sound enthusiastic, but her head had been too full of Max and Simon. Seeing them together like that had made her realize – she had to ask Max if she could meet her dad.

Max was still talking. 'Mrs Haynes showed me your work,' she said.

'Why did she do that?' Rain had wondered why Max and Mrs Haynes had gone off together, leaving her waiting with Simon in the car.

'Because I asked her,' Max said. 'She told me you're very clever, but I knew that already. She said you've caught up with the others even though you've never been to school. She said you could probably do just about anything you want with your life. I don't know how you've managed it, not with everything that's been happening. And I know I haven't helped much.'

Rain felt the tears in her eyes, but she blinked them away.

'I don't understand a lot of the stuff you've been doing,' Max said, 'but I can see how hard you've worked. You're good at all the things I was useless at.'

'I did tell you,' Rain said. 'I've told you lots of times.'

'I know. But I suppose I always thought that maybe one day . . .'

'What? I'd suddenly discover my artistic talent? You should see my pictures of fish.'

'I can imagine.'

'Max,' said Rain, her voice sounding too loud in her ears, 'I've decided something. I want to meet my dad.'

There was a long silence. Then Max said, 'You're sure?'

Rain nodded. 'I keep dreaming about it. I thought maybe we could meet him by the sea.'

Rain didn't tell Max how her dreams

always ended – with her losing Max in an endless maze of sand dunes.

Max made the arrangements. There was a phone call to Grandma that started off polite and ended up angry, and another one late at night when Rain was in bed. When it was over Max came into her room. 'Are you awake?' she asked quietly.

'Yes.'

Max sat down on the bed. 'It's all sorted. There's a place we both know, by the sea. We went there once when we were students.'

'When are we meeting him?'

'Not this Saturday, the one after.'

'Was it OK?' asked Rain. 'Talking to him, I mean.'

'It was weird. I didn't think I'd mind, but I still feel a bit shaky.'

'Thanks, Max.' Rain reached out in the darkness and felt for Max's hand. 'When we go and meet him,' she said, 'will you be all right? I mean, if you want . . . if Simon wants . . . maybe he could come too.'

And then, as Rain drifted into sleep, she heard Max humming one of the old songs, very softly, as if she was a little girl again.

* * *

'Rain,' called Max. 'Are you ready? It's time to go.'

Rain pulled herself out from underneath the engine and wiped her hands on a piece of rag. Saturday morning had finally arrived. She didn't know how she would have got through the two weeks' waiting if Max hadn't persuaded her to start working on the van.

She stood up stiffly. The bonnet was open and Tony Moore had his head buried in the engine. Simon had rigged up two sets of powerful lights for them to work by, but it was still very cold in the barn. Daniel's sisters were playing inside the bus while Daniel worked at smoothing over a patch of blue filler on the bottom of one of the doors. He was planning to copy some of the paintings from the bus onto the side of the van.

It had been Daniel's idea, asking his dad to help, and it was a good thing he had, because Rain knew she could never have fixed the van without him. And she knew it had been good for Tony and Daniel, too. They'd worked every evening for two weeks, and all weekend. Rain watched them standing together as Tony checked what Daniel had done. It seemed all wrong to Rain that

Daniel's family were so much happier now that Tony had left. Although – that wasn't quite right, she thought, as Daniel put his sandpaper down and pulled off his mask. Daniel might not be miserable any more, but there was still a kind of sadness about him. And it was the same with his mum, and with Tony. Only the three girls seemed untouched by what had happened to them. They were waving at her now, from the bus.

'Good luck then,' Daniel said.

'Thanks,' said Rain. 'I'd better go and get cleaned up.'

'It'll be OK,' Daniel told her. 'I know it will.'

'Come on,' Max said. 'We don't want to be late.'

Rain put her spanner back in the toolbox and followed Max outside. The morning was clear, but there was no warmth in the winter sun. 'I want to show you something before we go,' said Max. 'In the studio.'

Max opened the door and switched on the lights. Rain looked at the big painting hanging on the end wall, and she knew at once that it was finished, complete. From the black thunderclouds, a sheet of rain now fell across the sunlit marshes.

'What do you think?' asked Max.

Rain gazed at the picture. For months she'd watched it grow and change. It had become part of her life. She remembered those first pencil lines on the paper, the day of the football match, and then the day the whole canvas had turned red. You could still see the red, if you looked for it, but it was overlaid now with greens and browns and blacks. The painting *was* the marshes; it was a thunderstorm and sunlight. But it was more than that, too. It had come to life, and there were feelings in it, big feelings.

'You see,' said Max. 'You know, don't you? You can tell. You've always been the best judge, even when you were little.'

It was true, Rain thought, looking at the picture again. All through her life there had always been a picture growing. And she'd always been able to tell when they were finished.

Max hugged her. 'Now go and get changed,' she said. 'Simon will be here any minute.'

Rain took off the dirty overalls and pulled on a couple of her oldest, most precious jumble sale jumpers. Then she stood in front of the mirror and looked at herself, trying to imagine what her dad would think when he saw her. She'd grown, and the torn, faded jeans that had been so baggy in the summer were barely long enough now. The jumpers and shirts, too, seemed to have shrunk. Her hair was still short and spiky. Max had cut it the night before, and she'd put all her earrings back. That had been hard. She hadn't worn them since she'd started school, and the holes had nearly closed up, but she'd got them all in eventually. She reached up and briefly touched her small blue sapphire, then she turned and ran down the stairs.

Max and Simon were waiting. 'Hey,' said Simon. 'You look great. Exactly how you looked the day I first saw you.'

Rain saw that Simon had his arm around Max's waist. She didn't think she'd ever get used to seeing them like that. She tried to hide the way she felt, but Max must have noticed something in her face, because she moved away from Simon and picked up the map from the table. 'OK,' she said. 'Let's do it then.'

*   *   *

'Not far now,' said Max, turning round to look at her. The winter landscape was still rolling past the car window, fields of washed-out brown and green, the hedges and the leafless trees. But now, across the fields, Rain saw a ruined church, its tower sticking up like a broken tooth, and a flash of light that might be the sea. 'How are you feeling?' Max asked her.

'Nervous.'

'You still want to do it? I could ring him.'

Rain shook her head, but she smiled, in spite of her churning stomach. These days Max never went anywhere without her phone. 'You're sure?' said Max, turning round again.

But Rain didn't reply because Simon was stopping the car. They were in a lane and the ruined church was beside them. Ahead, the lane ran on a little way and seemed to end in sky. They got out of the car and the wind tugged at their clothes. Rain saw a man standing by another car that was parked on the grassy verge further down the lane, and she gripped Max's hand tightly.

He was tall, taller than he had looked in the photographs. His hair was cropped very short, and his face was serious as he walked towards them. Rain couldn't move, or speak. 'Hello, Rain,' he said. 'This is weird, isn't it?' He smiled, and Rain found herself smiling, too, although she felt that at any moment she might start to cry.

'I . . . I don't know what to call you,' she said.

'Cameron will do fine,' he told her. He looked at Max. 'It's been a long time.'

Max nodded and there was an awkward pause. 'This is Simon,' Max said at last. Simon and Cameron shook hands, then Cameron turned back to Rain. 'What shall we do?' he asked her. 'Shall we go for a walk?'

Rain looked at Max. 'It's up to you,' Max said. 'We'll wait in the car. Or we'll come if you like?'

Rain shook her head. She knew Max understood. This was one thing she really did have to do on her own. She walked down the lane beside her dad and then the land stopped abruptly on the edge of a cliff, a jagged edge of tarmac jutting out into the air. 'We can't get down here,' Cameron said. 'We walk that way, along the cliff. The sea's eating the land away. Hundreds of years ago there used to be a whole town out there, where the sea is now.'

Rain looked. You would never have known. Below them, waves crashed on a deserted beach. 'So the bus finally packed up, then?' Cameron said as they walked along the crumbling cliffs.

'You saw it then,' asked Rain, 'when Max got it?'

'We bought it together. She must have told you about that? No. I suppose she wouldn't have. In fact, it might even have been my idea.'

'I didn't know.'

'The thing is,' Cameron went on, 'I thought living in a bus was a great idea for a couple of young artists. We'd travel around the country painting and drawing. Go where we liked, even abroad if we wanted to.'

'And?'

'And then you came along, Rain, that's what. I didn't see how it could work, not with a baby. But Max thought different.' He stopped for a moment, looking out to sea. 'But I suppose she was right, after all. I mean, it's worked out fine, hasn't it?' When Rain didn't reply, he continued: 'Max is doing brilliantly with the paintings, even if your grandma doesn't like them. And look at you. And it worked out for me, too. I've got a great family. That's what I wanted to say. I mean . . . you can be part of it . . . if you want. In a way you're part of it already.'

There was a gap in the cliffs where the sea had eaten them away. There was a gap in her life too. An emptiness. 'But you weren't *there*,' she said. She didn't know where the words came from.

'What?' Cameron's face was blank.

'All that time, when we were travelling around in the bus. It was good. I'm not saying it wasn't. Most of the time. But you weren't there. You weren't there and nothing you do now can ever change that.'

Suddenly Rain thought of Daniel and Tony. Things were difficult between them but she knew they loved each other, they were tied together by all those years they'd been together. It was the same with them as it was with her and Max. It would never be like that with the stranger who stood in front of her.

Cameron swallowed. The bleached trunk of a fallen tree lay nearby on the beach, half-buried by sand, and he sat on it. 'I would have kept in touch,' he said. 'I wanted to send money. But Max didn't want that. You know what she's like. I shouldn't think she's changed. Everything was black and white. Max said . . .' He stopped. 'You don't need to know all this.'

'But I do,' Rain told him. 'That's the whole point.'

'We can't change the past, though, can we? And there are things that only Max can explain to you. But listen, Rain. I know you're upset . . .'

She opened her mouth to speak, but he waved her to silence. 'OK,' he said, 'maybe upset isn't a big enough word for it. But there's something you have to understand. What happened between me and Max – it was nobody's fault. There's no one to blame. Sometimes people like each other a lot, like me and Max, but in the end they're just not cut out to live together. I wish I could have been around for you. I really do. I . . .' He stopped. He was crying.

'I'm sorry,' Rain whispered. 'I didn't think it would be like this.' She walked away from him, right down to the edge of the sea. This was nothing like her dreams. Waves wet her shoes but she didn't notice. A cloud passed in front of the sun and the sea was cold and grey. She turned and looked back. Her dad was still sitting on the fallen tree, watching her. She walked up the beach towards him, her feet slipping in the wet shingle. 'Please,' she said, 'can we go back now?'

They walked back along the cliff top in silence. When they reached the lane again, Rain said, 'Your daughter . . . does she really look like me?'

'Very much. You are sisters after all. Half-sisters anyhow. I'd really like them to meet you, you know.'

'I can't,' said Rain. 'Not yet.'

'No. I can see that. But . . . I will see you again, won't I?'

The question hung between them, unanswered. They had reached Simon's car, but it was empty. Rain heard the sound of Max's laughter coming from the old church. The arches of the windows framed the sky. 'Max seems happy,' Cameron said. 'Simon seems like a nice man.'

They walked towards the gap where the church door had been. When they reached it Rain saw that the crumbling flint walls had nothing but lumpy grass inside them. The grass was nibbled short like a lawn by rabbits. Their droppings were everywhere. At the far end of the space, under the remains of the tall east window, Max and Simon were sitting.

'I won't stay,' Cameron said to Rain. He waved to Max.

Rain looked up at him, and for the first time she saw something of herself in him, in his sad eyes, in the way he smiled. It was the same for both of them, she knew.

'Well, this is it then . . .'

Cameron paused. 'Look . . . about meeting again . . . I . . .'

But Rain stopped him. 'I don't know,' she said. 'I don't really know about anything. Not any more.'

'I'm sorry. I shouldn't have asked. Not yet. It's too soon.'

'No. It's OK. I mean . . . maybe . . .'

He hesitated, then held his hand towards her. She reached out and took it. She saw the black oil stains around her fingernails, felt a warm, dry squeeze, the touch of his skin, and then he was gone. She watched him walk to his car, watched him as he drove away, and then she turned back to Max and Simon, who were waiting quietly under the tall window full of clouds and sunshine.

Rain gazed at Max's face through the flames. They had made the fire with driftwood, and it hissed and crackled as it burned. Tiny fires were reflected in Max's eyes. Above their heads the black sky of the longest night of the year was thick with stars. The thunder of the surf roared in Rain's ears.

'Are you glad we came?' asked Max.

'Of course. Aren't you?'

Max nodded, staring into the flames. The old Max back again, thought Rain, the wild Max, the one she'd grown up with. Only, this Max had always been there, inside. Daniel had seen it, even when she couldn't. Daniel had *drawn* it. He'd love it here. One day she'd bring him, maybe. But this time it was just her and Max, the way it always had been.

Max had appeared outside the school on the last day of term driving the half-painted van. 'What are you doing here?' Rain said.

'Magical mystery tour. It's the shortest day tomorrow, so we're going away. OK?'

'But my stuff . . .'

'All packed. Get in. There's a long way to go.'

Rain climbed into the van and they drove off. The last thing she saw was Daniel, waving. She waved back, and at the same moment she heard something hit the side of the van. She looked out of the opposite window and saw Stephen standing on the pavement with his friends. A plastic lemonade bottle was rolling back across the road.

'Some things will never change,' Max said.

'You don't know that.'

Max glanced sideways at her. 'Yeah, well,' she said. 'We'll find out, won't we?'

Max drove all night while Rain slept. She stopped in the car park of a motorway service station at dawn and they climbed out and stretched, smelling the clean moorland air blowing down from the rounded hills behind them. After breakfast, Max slept for a few hours on the mattress in the back of the van, and then they drove on, through Glasgow and on up into the mountains. Rain watched the familiar scenery unfolding in front of her. It seemed like another lifetime when they had last been here, but it was only a few short months ago. The hills had been green then, where now they were every shade of brown, and increasingly, as they drove further north, capped with snow. It started raining as they crossed a loch on a small ferry and drove onwards along ever narrower, bendier roads. When they finally parked by the side of the rocky bay the clouds seemed to be touching the sea, and there was no sign of the mountainous islands that Rain knew were out there.

'It was like this the day you were born,' said Max, as they sat in the van with steaming mugs of soup in their hands, listening to the sound of the rain drumming on the roof. Rain knew the story, but she never minded hearing it again. It was how she'd got her name, after all. 'I drove into the hospital car park,' Max went on, 'and I honked the horn. I must have been in labour for hours and not realized. This young doctor came in through the door and I told him you were about to arrive, and he said, "Don't be silly." I can still hear his voice. Then he looked and he said, "My God, I can see the head!" Someone else had arrived by then and they got me on the back seat, and that's where you were born. I wanted to stay in the bus, but they wouldn't let me. They weren't too happy about letting me take you off afterwards, either. They sent social workers and everything, but they couldn't stop me.'

'I'm glad,' said Rain.

'Are you? Really?'

'Yes.'

'You don't wish you'd had an ordinary life? A house and a car and school and friends?'

'It's all there, inside me. All my life with you. Nothing will take it away.' Rain paused. 'Max, you didn't mind me seeing my dad, did you? Only, sometimes I think . . .'

'It was hard,' Max said. 'Of course it was hard. He . . . he was worse than any of them, you know, back then. It was like he wanted to own me . . . and you too. But I could see that you had to do it. And really, now I've seen him again, I suppose he's not that bad.'

There was a long silence. 'You love Simon,

don't you?' said Rain. Her voice didn't seem to be working properly.

'Yes,' said Max. Her voice was so quiet Rain could hardly hear it. 'Yes, I think I do.'

Rain felt her face crumpling. She didn't know why she was crying. She had a stupid cup of soup in her hands. Max took it from her and held her. 'Listen to me,' she said fiercely. 'You don't have to share me with him. It's not like that. You're my daughter. I love you, Rain. Don't ever think I don't love you. OK?'

They sat for a long time, watching the grey sky and the sea. And then, gradually, the cloud began to lift and the wind dropped. 'Come on,' Max said. 'Time to light a fire.'

They walked along the white sand collecting driftwood. Out at sea, the islands appeared slowly from the gloom, black against the sky. Max set fire to the small pile of kindling they had brought with them, and as the darkness grew they piled more and more driftwood onto the flames, so that now there was real heat to warm them, in spite of the coldness of the winter night.

'From now on,' Max said, 'it just gets

better. Every day there's more light. It'll soon be spring.'

Rain looked at the blaze and felt her heart lift. This was why they had come. She looked beyond the flames, out into the wild darkness, and felt the rock beneath her feet. Somehow, knowing all this was here made everything else seem more possible. The new year would come, and she would find the strength to see her dad again, and maybe meet his family, her brother and her sisters. She would survive school, somehow. She would even learn to live with Simon. There would be other things too, things she couldn't even begin to imagine. Her whole life stretched out in front of her . . .

A piece of wood crackled and fell into the fire. A shower of sparks rose into the blackness and Rain laughed at herself. She had the sea and the rocks, the fire and the night full of stars. She had Max.

And, right now, that was enough.

GREEN FINGERS
by Paul May

'That's all I am — a problem!'

Kate doesn't want to leave the city and move into
a tatty old farmhouse out in the middle of nowhere.
She knows that, no matter what Mum and Dad
say, it's *her* fault the family needs a 'fresh start' -
her problems at school.

But the move doesn't seem to solve anything. Dad's
DIY disasters mean Mum and Dad are arguing even
more than before, and Kate finds her new school just
as frustrating as ever as she tries to piece together the
puzzle that is reading. Then she meets Walter, their
curmudgeonly old neighbour, and discovers a *new*
puzzle. For buried beneath the overgrown weeds
behind their house is a wonderful garden — a garden
just waiting to be put together again ...

An engrosssing tale of individuality, trouble —
and a very special talent.

0 440 864569

DEFENDERS
Paul May

'Who wants to watch other people score all the goals?'

Chris is a goalscorer – but his life is a mess.
He's falling out with everyone: his dad, his teachers,
even his best mate. There's just one good thing
left - banging the ball into the back of the net.
So even if his school team *does* need defenders,
Chris won't play if he can't be up front...

Joe is a new boy. He reckons Chris is a natural
in defence and should give it a go. And Joe knows
about defenders. He's been watching the best
all his life – his dad...

Ian Rawson is Joe's dad. An ex-Premier League
defender, he's absolute *magic* on the pitch, in
total control of the game...

When Chris sees Ian play, he starts to wonder.
Has he got it all wrong? And if he changes his
mind, will there still be a place for him in the team?

A terrific, action-packed soccer story from
the author of *Troublemakers.*

CORGI YEARLING BOOKS

ISBN 0 440 864429

TROUBLEMAKERS
Paul May

Tough enough for the team?

Robbie is desperate to try out for the school football team. He's full of raw talent, skilful and agile, with terrific co-ordination. So why does everybody reckon he's got no chance?

Chester Smith is a top-class professional United player. But his game is falling to pieces, and now he's faced with a continual barrage of ugly taunts from ignorant hooligans in the crowd...

Then Robbie and Chester meet, and it could be the beginning of a new chance for each of them. If only they can avoid the troublemakers...

An action-packed football tale, *Troublemakers* is hard-hitting, realistic and inspiring.

SHORTLISTED FOR THE BRANFORD BOASE AWARD 2000

CORGI YEARLING BOOKS

ISBN 0 440 864194

RESCUING DAD
Pete Johnson

'How do you improve your dad?'

Joe and Claire can see why Mum chucked Dad
out. He looks a mess, he can't cook and he's
useless around the house. Something must be done:
they're the only ones who can help transform him
into 'Dad Mark Two'. And when they unveil this
new, improved dad, Mum will be so impressed
she'll take him back on the spot!

But then disaster strikes – Mum starts seeing the
slimy and creepy Roger. And Joe and Claire's plans
take an unexpected turn – with hilarious results.

'Pete Johnson is a wonderful story-teller'
Evening Standard

'An author of exceptional talents…sensitive,
humorous and down-to-earth' *The School Librarian*

CORGI YEARLING BOOKS

ISBN 0 440 864577